Norky Is Still Ram

Norky's Ramblings book two.

Peter Norcliffe.

Table of Contents

Table of Contents.. 2

Dedication.. 4

Acknowledgements.. 5

About the Author.. 8

Introduction.. 9

Chapter 1: The swinging 60s.. 10

Chapter 2: My driving test and biking mates...................................... 16

Chapter 3: Grandchildren or lack thereof... 23

Chapter 4: Train spotting.. 25

Chapter 5: The Norcliffe ancestry... 31

Chapter 6: How the other half lives, or at least try to live................. 37

Chapter 7: Musical performances.. 41

Chapter 8: Slowly becoming more civilised... 48

Chapter 9: Medical interventions.. 53

Chapter 10: Accidents happen.. 57

Chapter 11: The Wakefield Bierkeller beginning of another

adventure... 63

Chapter 12: Lovely ladies... 67

Chapter 13: In search of the B17 (bucket list)..................................... 74

Chapter 14: Do men ever really grow up?.. 78

Chapter 15: The parachute jump (bucket list)...................................... 83

Chapter 16: Arrival of Rachel... 89

Chapter 17: At last ticking off the B17 from the bucket list................. 94

Chapter 18: Three day week, banter, nicknames and pranks............... 98

Chapter 19: Beers and Pubs.. 103

Chapter 20: The Devil's music.. 108

Chapter 21: A Luddite and proud.................................... 115

Chapter 22: Bike tours part one, with friends.................. 120

Chapter 23: Bike tours part two, on our own................... 126

Chapter 24: Huddersfield Narrow Canal......................... 133

Chapter 25: Likes, dislikes and how habits change........... 138

Chapter 26: Music in Yorkshire...................................... 143

Chapter 27: More tours by motorcycle, this time to Poland... 148

Chapter 28: Krakow and Auschwitz Birkenau................. 153

Chapter 29: Childhood procedures soothed by jelly and ice cream..... 170

Chapter 30: Cost of living in 1947, Jammin' an' things on t' telly.......... 174

Chapter 31: The big screen and family fallouts................ 179

Chapter 32: A W.A.R.T.S. walk to St. Aidan's.................. 184

Chapter 33: How Yorkshire helped to shape the modern world.......... 190

Chapter 34: Memories and thoughts following another W.A.R.T.S.
           walk.. 195

Chapter 35: Be proud of your accents............................. 200

Chapter 36: Community service and home-front support....... 204

Chapter 37: Danger ramble... 209

Chapter 38: Write it down for future generations or just for a
           good read.. 214

Chapter 39: Mary Norcliffe nee Holdsworth, my life and times........... 216

Chapter 40: Local sites and regular visitors to Golcar and
           Bolster moor... 226

Chapter 41: Time to talk about prostates......................... 232

Dedication

Again I have to dedicate this book to my wife Moira
and our daughter Rachel, who continue to find the energy
to encourage this ramble.
However, the initial blame still sits squarely on the shoulders
of our good friend Frances Cole
who was the initiator and is fully responsible.

Acknowledgements

I also continue to draw on inspiration and the memory of my big sister Rhondda and brother Nick. My brother-in-law John was also a great contributor with memory and photos included in chapter 20, "Devils Music". The continued friendship and inspiration from my best mates in the W.A.R.T.S. walking group including in alphabetical order to eliminate unpleasantness, Bev, Hester, Michael, Nick, Paul, Peter and part-time junior member Rachel.

Louise Houghton from Yorkshire Bylines, the on-line magazine, has continued to publish many of my ramblings, and together with the sub editors The Lovely Helen Johnson and Sean Dadds, continue to educate me in the English language and drag me kicking and screaming into a mind-set and opinion that is acceptable in this modern confusing world we live in. Unfortunately they are not always successful and I can often slip back into my slovenly ways and will get a gentle reminder which of course I fully accept for their magazine. However, many of my comments and opinions they may have edited out have magically found themselves back into this book.

Hester our W.A.R.T.S. Colonel was kind enough to write this following review, and it is so good that I felt compelled to include it somewhere in this book.

> *"It's not often that a good yarn spinner emerges these days without a literary pedigree. We'll search online for an ancestry that embraces graduation with honours from creative writing courses, appearances on stage at storytelling festivals or, at the very least, a hint of struggle and dedication, a slew of rejection slips before fame and recognition reward persistence and belief.*

Peter's own route to publication has none of these. Leaving school with an aversion to education, and to reading in particular, he embarked on a life lived very much in the present. A beneficiary of the post war employment boom he rocked with the fifties and swung with the sixties, taking the world as he found it and making plenty of mistakes on the way. He has never had any ambition for fortune, has lived a life of steady employment but always in factories of his own choosing, has married young and well and raised a family, all within a few square miles of a small patch of Huddersfield.

But what school overlooked, that sharp intelligence, that ability to hold an audience with humour, humility and self depreciation is found on every page of this collection of tales from his younger and not so younger years .

Here we find a world familiar to many but now as arcane as ginnels, back boilers, flat caps and pints of mild. A world less innocent and wholesome than the nostalgia industry would have us believe but where family, neighbours and workmates live, eat and play within a mucky landscape written on by a century of industrial might. Mill, mines and terraces rising and falling across moorland and valley. Dirty rivers and canals. Trolley buses and two wheels instead of four, sometimes powered with fascinating internal combustion engines. And lots of smoke, dust and congestion

I came to this valley a fresh faced family doctor nearly forty years ago and it was An Event . People queued to see their first Lady Doctor, inventing maladies and sharing impressions over yard walls. I paid courtesy calls to the clergy, the policeman, the club stewards, publicans and the undertaker. It was the undertaker who captured the spirit of the place. He took me out of the silent carpeted office and onto his doorstep with the broad sweep of industry below us, the roads weaving their warp and weft between the houses.

"What you're looking at is the last of village England," he said. I didn't understand him. It was as far away from a village as I could imagine. I thought he might be slightly touched. But, after a few months in the job, witnessing the extraordinary sense of family, place and connection that bound everyone together I got it. And understood my place in it.

Huddersfield isn't a chocolate box town, is no longer wealthy and was never desirable. It wears it's past glories in the soot coating the golden sandstone of its buildings and in the hard humour of adversity. But Peter's stories make you glad to know the place and spend some time here. Enjoy them. Enjoy the company. It's like spending time with a good friend".

Doctor Hester Dunlop. GP.

I filled up when I first read this. We become complacent with many of the things we live with from childhood and it sometimes takes something like this review, or encouragement from family and friends to make us realise how privileged we are.

Many thanks must also go to Pam Dimbleby for finalising and layout work, Chris Friend and Rachel Norcliffe for their initial editing and Malcolm Laverty (Stan) for the front cover image.

About the author

Artwork by Stan

Peter Norcliffe is a proud Yorkshireman, he does not suffer fools gladly and is now old enough to walk away from fools without allowing them to effect him more than is necessary, usually that is. Peter is sociable and equally happy in groups or in a quiet corner on his own. Qualities taught to him by his parents Clifford and Mary Norcliffe, who while he was a child encouraged him to seek adventure in his surroundings of Bolster Moor and Golcar and knew not to stifle his natural boisterous spirit which would have been difficult in the extreme, particularly if he hadn't been fed.

Introduction

This book is a continued journey through the fog of my memory, and as with book one, "Norky's Ramblings", it includes stories, anecdotes and tales short and tall, from friends, family but mostly of my own. All the stories are true, as far as memory and adequate research has allowed. Even the stories that may appear to be a tale taller than the ordinary are still true, mostly, no really they are, honest.

There is no start, middle or end to this book. The only chronological order that this book may have is that each chapter appears in the book in the order that they sprang into my mind.

A topic would jump into my head and I would sit down at the keyboard and start writing before the memory drifted into the ether, but within just a few lines my train of thought would shoot off in an entirely different direction, a process which I still find fascinating, and of course, why the books are a ramble.

Chapter 1: The swinging 60s

The 'swinging sixties' may or may not have existed. If it did, it never swung through Huddersfield. We were still recovering from the excitement of running water, indoor bathrooms, and electricity. London and perhaps Liverpool and Manchester may have felt its presence, but if it made any attempt to enter Yorkshire, I didn't notice.

During my early youth, when couples came together, they expected – and were expected – to spend a lifetime of love, devotion and commitment to their relationship. There was a hope, if not expectation, that both were virginal, or at least appeared or claimed to be so. Finding such a partner was relatively straightforward and not all that uncommon, since at the time abstinence was the only reliable form of birth control.

If the relationship blossomed and the young man appeared committed to marriage, offered a promise of life-long support of ageing grandparents or at least loved cats, then there was an increasing probability that this relationship would blossom into a passionate bonding and a special cuddle of the type Mums told you nothing about.

If that happened, it was the young man's responsibility to ensure pregnancy was avoided. Condoms were available of course, but only in very limited outlets – barbers and the chemists being the only reliable source. There was your Jack-the-lad mate who always seemed to have some, so you might choose to pay an inflated price and hope that you'd also appear to be a Jack-the-lad, but then find that the 'best by date' was the previous year.

Still, it was kept in your wallet anyway, and when the wallet was changed the condom was still there. That's when you realised that the condom was lasting longer than your leather wallet. Buying condoms was guaranteed to involve embarrassment. The classic 1962 film A kind of Loving starring Alan Bates, shows him entering a chemist to buy condoms but once inside he becomes overwhelmingly embarrassed and leaves with a bottle of Lucozade instead.

The whole subject of sex was embarrassing for the parents and confusing for the children. I remember asking Mum what certain round-shaped bits of my lower anatomy were for. I'd have been about 35 years old I think (or probably nearer nine or ten). Mum said, "I don't know, ask your dad". So I did, but Dad also said "I don't know".

That was the end of my sex education until the morning of my wedding. Moi had had a miscarriage a few weeks earlier, but Dad still felt it his duty to take me to one side and quietly ask, "Do you know how babies are made?" Even though Dad had spent nearly five years at sea fighting the dastardly Germans, he seemed very relieved when I told him that I knew enough to get by.

That's the story of many aspects of my life really – just knowing enough to get by.

One of the ways to meet a future life-long partner was a Saturday afternoon stroll around Huddersfield town centre with our mates. The girls would wash their hair in the morning and as hair dryers were not readily available, they fitted huge curlers and covered the whole thing with a scarf.

Us chaps would perhaps catch the eye of a girl and practise our pathetic chat-up lines. It's a wonder any of us got a second glance. That was another responsibility for the chaps: they had to do the chatting up. The nearest that a young woman may have got to initiate the chat-up would go something like "My mate fancies your mate" and a complicated go-between would follow.

We'd make arrangements to meet that night outside Woolies (Woolworths) or if we were feeling posh, Rushworth's department store.

If we had taken the time to look through the Friday night's Examiner, we could also decide on about a dozen local cinemas, at least six in the town centre alone. Again, if we wanted to impress, we would suggest meeting outside the ABC cinema on Market Street. Originally called the Ritz Cinema it became the ABC in 1961, but we still referred to it as 'The Ritz'. It was closed in 1983 and demolished soon after.

The problems we often found when meeting the young woman that we'd first met only a few hours earlier was that we couldn't recognise them, as their appearance had drastically changed. They were wearing posh frocks and Saturday night makeup, but the biggest difference was the hair. It was often backcombed to within an inch of its life and dominated the whole head and surrounding district.

*This photo appeared in a Great Yarmouth newspaper in 1965.
Moi was writing home and her friend Maureen was
checking for spelling mistakes.*

*Saturday afternoon look. Moi (on the left) again with her friend Maureen
favoured straight hair and a big fringe, so stuck theirs down with Sellotape.
Except when they didn't of course, all very confusing.
This was a good example of "my mate fancies your mate": Maureen and my
mate Dave have been married for almost as long as Moi and I have.*

On our Saturday afternoon strolls we would inevitably migrate to the music shops where we could meet a girl. We could also ask to listen to a particular record. One of the staff would place the record on one of several turntables behind the counter and then we were told which booth to use.

Perhaps we could get three people in the booth, which was the size of an old telephone box. Woods music shop was a bit posh, and they would only let us listen to two records before throwing us out. They didn't like young chaps and thought rock and roll was the work of the Devil anyway. On the other hand, WH Smith's had a very pleasant assistant called Beverley working behind the counter, and she let us listen to as many as we wanted without buying.

Crow Lane Youth Club was a very popular meeting place for us. We could play cards, chess, badminton, table tennis and watch our favourite television programmes of the time, then we would venture on to the pub.

It may seem odd that a youth club catered for young people old enough to go to pubs, but the age ranged from about 15 to 20 years old. The youth leaders were Pat (Patrick) and Sylvia, both very capable, pleasant and go-to people for help and guidance. There was very little aggravation in the club, but if there was, it was easily sorted out by Pat, an ex-boxer of Irish descent.

Crow Lane sometimes had live local groups, of which there were many. Guitar and drum groups were becoming well established, with many rock and roll songs coming to Britain from the USA, all needing 2/3 guitars, a set of drums and a singer.

The music establishment, from the likes of Woods Music Shop to the BBC, assumed it was only going to be a fad, hence the popularity of Radio Caroline and Radio Luxembourg. The BBC was eventually dragged kicking and screaming into the modern world, and in 1967, forced to compete with the pirate and commercial radio stations, launched Radio One.

Traditional ballroom dance halls had been available in Huddersfield for generations, and still are. But in the 50s and 60s the Devil's dance – jiving – was taking root, as was the wearing of skirts that revealed the stocking tops. And that was just the chaps.

Of course, there were plenty of parties, and there may have been alcohol involved; I was above that sort of thing of course.

When my parents moved from the Golcar council estate after they bought the chippy (fish and chip shop) in Birkby, I was also allowed to join them. Being only 15 years old they perhaps thought I was a little young to be sent out into the world just yet.

However, my place of work was then more than three miles and two bus journeys away. Dad said as soon as I became old enough, he would buy me a motorbike – very much in the family tradition. To his credit, soon after my 16th birthday in 1963, he did. In those days, and until 1972, a full motorcycle driving licence was allowed at that age.

Chapter 2: My driving test and biking mates

Driving licences had been compulsory since 1903, but this only meant applying for a licence locally – no need for insurance, road fund licence or test certificate. The only stipulation was that the applicant had to be 17 years old, except when applying for a motorcycle licence.

Requirements gradually changed. Insurance and tax were first to be introduced, and then in 1934 a driving test. Other changes followed when the first motorway, the Preston Bypass (now part of the M6), opened in 1958. In 1972, many new motorcycle laws were introduced, including changing the age requirements for over 50cc bikes from 16 to 17 years old.

This was brought about because the Japanese motorcycle manufacturers, mainly Honda, were producing very fast bikes. We were all very scathing about them, Calling them "jap crap", very UNPC now of course. In reality they were fantastic bikes, much quicker and much more reliable than our Triumph, BSA, Norton, Velocette, Ariel, Matchless, Royal Enfield and Vincent motorcycles could ever be.

Triumph are the only British motorcycle manufacturers left. They decided many years ago to take the Japanese on at their own game, and they have done an excellent job. After several set-backs during their revival in the late 70s and early 80s, they invested in a much more modern manufacturing system and now produce a range of performance and touring bikes to rival any manufacturer.

My first bike was a BSA C10L, a 250cc side valve single, which on a good day would have no problem 'pulling the skin off a rice pudding', a common expression for rating the power, strength or lack thereof. As most idiot lads do, I took my Beeza (BSA) on a road to test it out at its maximum.

My chosen road was a downhill section of the road into Elland. I set off, soon getting into top gear. Laying flat along the top of the bike, my chin firmly pressed into the petrol tank, arse up, head down, elbows and knees tucked in. The rush of air told me that I must be reaching some sort of maximum velocity. I imagined myself to be my heroes Mike Hailwood or John Surtees.

As I reached my treasured terminal velocity, I bravely lifted my head into the hurricane to see what the speedometer was registering: 65 miles an hour. Can't be, I said, but further tests proved it to be true. It had to go.

Norky in late summer 1963, proudly presenting his 250cc BSA C10L. Side valve.

The words 'skin', 'could not', 'pudding', 'rice', 'pull off', immediately sprang to mind.

Soon after this photo was taken I passed my test, which wasn't difficult in those days. The test observer just watched from the pavement, and the emergency stop was instigated by him (it was always a him) quickly raising his hand. Some very brave observers stepped out in front of the rider – mine did not. He could probably see the mad glint in my eye. I knew nobody who admitted to failing their bike test. I think the only time we would fail was when the observer was run over, and even then, if he was able to regain his feet, you still had a chance.

Just a few of the fine group of friends. I think I could honestly say that there were perhaps only two potentially loose cannons.

But they grew up just in time.

I had by this time met with an established group of bikers and one said that their mate Baz was selling his bike. On further investigation I discovered that it was Baz's father that was selling the bike while Baz was on holiday. His dad was very concerned that he would soon kill himself if he carried on with biking.

Both Baz and his dad were very good mechanics and had tuned and adapted a Triumph Tiger 100 to look and perform like the classic Bonneville, and it was fast. I was 16 years old, owned one of the fastest bikes in Huddersfield, and had a cocky, arrogant attitude that dictated that I was eventually going to get into trouble with the police or killed. Luckily in some ways, it was the former. I can still remember some of the detailed tuning, alloy splayed twin carb cylinder head and matching alloy barrel, two one inch Amal carburettors, 9 to 1 compression pistons and E3134 high lift cams. Baz had made the engine and the bike itself look and perform like the classic Triumph Bonneville.

Memory works in very mysterious ways, why do I after more than 50 years remember these details, even the E3134 serial number is forever etched in my tiny memory, I can't remember the most basic......................ah...........words, but I'll even write it again E3134 just to prove that I can, it just rolls off the tongue somehow.

Between 16 and 19 I had many experiences of which I am not particularly proud. I received many points on my driving licence and I was eventually banned four times, from periods ranging from one to six months. There was one court appearance where I recognised the magistrate and hoped he didn't recognise me. No such luck. He looked at me and said, "Weren't you in this court last week?" I had to admit that I was, so that conversation resulted in another ban, of course.

The bike and I had become "known" to the police. I eventually had to sell it to pay for food and fines. I was told that the lad who bought the bike was pulled over by the police, and as he approached the poor unsuspecting lad, the police officer said, "Right, Norcliffe isn't it?"

I was pulled over many times, at least once a month. It was a thing many bikers had to put up with in those days. It wasn't difficult for the police to find something amiss. Most of my misdemeanours were for "driving without due care, no road tax, and no insurance". Strangely, I was never caught speeding or drink driving.

Even though I'm not proud of my cocky, arrogant attitude of that time, I gained a friendship with many fantastic lads and lasses, many of whom I still see. Unfortunately, as we were born in the forties, many of our good friends are no longer with us. We all get together in our local club every six months or so to reminisce and to exaggerate old stories, (the older we get, the better we were) but the numbers are falling each year.

Luckily In mid 1965, I had started a regular relationship with the lovely Moi, and she somehow became pregnant. Doing the gentlemanly thing, I ran away. No I didn't. Arrangements were made for our wedding in December 1966. Unfortunately, Moi had a miscarriage before the wedding, but we knew we were meant for each other, and also that this was our opportunity to commit to a relatively stable life and to get ourselves out of the less-than-perfect situation we (particularly me) were in.

December 26th 1966. Mr. Hallam was the vicar of Longwood Church,
a lovely chap.

Moi's wedding dress was borrowed and my suit cost £12.00
and lasted about six months.

Materially we had nothing. We rented a flat over an empty shop in the next village. We were given an old, abandoned gas cooker that had been stored in a shed, an old moth-eaten couch, Moi's bed from home, and spare cutlery, crockery and linen. Wedding presents were a re-conditioned washing machine and a new – yes, new – iron and a set of pans and bed sheets. We had less than £10 in savings and cash. Luckily, I had completed my fines and driving bans and we both had a job. And, more importantly, we were happy.

Various stayes of happiness
over the last 56 years.
The willingness to dress-up
may help in that regard.

Chapter 3: Grandchildren, or lack thereof

I was talking to my cousin Roderick the other day and the subject of grandchildren came up, or to be more precise the lack thereof. Our maternal grandparents, Granddad and Grandma Holdsworth, had four children and 13 grandchildren; of those 13 cousins or siblings that have descended from the Holdsworths we have collectively only produced six grandchildren. I suspect this has much to do with how women are now more able to financially support themselves and can choose whether or not to have children.

I spent many happy times with my cousins, particularly the McInnes brothers. We were similar in ages, and they lived just a few hundred yards down the road. They were living at Westwood when we lived at Headwall Green and then we all moved to the new Sycamore Avenue council estate.

As the McInnes brothers were all encouraged to read, they always had lots of comics in the house such as Beano with Dennis the Menace and his dog Gnasher, Lord Snooty and Mouldy Oldie. They also had The Dandy with Desperate Dan with his cow pie, Corky the Cat and Black Bob. But my favourite was The Eagle with Dan Dare, the pilot of the future.

This had lots of inspiring picture stories about WW2, often featuring outnumbered brave British commandoes fighting dastardly Germans, who had little balloons above their heads with words like 'Himmel' or 'Donner und Blitzen' when they got what was coming to them.

As I was a very poor reader, I was more inspired by the pictures. In some ways I could make up my own stories but it usually wasn't necessary.

Just as inspiring was the true story of a British soldier William (Bill) Millin. He had been ordered by his commanding officer, Lord Lovat, to play the bagpipes along the beach on the first day of the D Day landings on 6 June 1944. Bill Millin was Lord Lovat's personal piper. This was designed to inspire his comrades of the Special Service Brigade, who were to support the paratroop regiment who had just taken Pegasus Bridge.

Bill could be seen marching up the Normandy beach playing renditions of songs such as 'Highland Laddie', clad in kilt and armed with no more than his dagger tucked into his sock. The German machine gunners and snipers could also see Bill, but the captured German soldiers later told him that they didn't want to shoot at him because they thought he was mad. Well, he was from Glasgow! Bill went on to have a full life and died in 2010 at the ripe old age of 88. It makes you proud to be British.

Chapter 4: Train spotting

In 1962, in pursuit of our train spotting hobby, Roderick, Peter and I cycled to York. (Boys tend to have these geeky hobbies – stamp collecting is another.) This was how I remembered it anyway. On further investigation, I recently asked Roderick, and Peter, the friend who I thought was with us when we cycled to York that day, and they remembered nothing of it. Memory is a funny thing, and obviously very poor in Roderick and Peter's case. However, in an attempt to rationalise my memory, and adding the input from Roderick and Peter, I decided, as it is a long way to cycle from Huddersfield to York when I was only 14/15, I/we must have only cycled part way and gone on the rest of the way by train.

We were going there primarily to see how many A4 Pacific's we could see. Nicknamed 'Streaks', A4 Pacific's were fully streamlined, and in my humble opinion the most beautiful, steam locos. We never got to see them on our line through the Colne Valley, so we had to go to places like Leeds and York. Designed by Sir Nigel Gresley, there were only 35 of these locos built.

We saw six that day, and like all young boys at the time we had to touch each nameplate. They were quite high, so we usually needed a little help. We would then underline the numbers in our train spotters' book compiled by the likes of Ian Allan. We could spend all day there after first paying 1p for our day platform ticket.

There are only six A4 Pacific's remaining. All the rest were scrapped, save one that was destroyed during the Baedeker air raids in 1942. (Baedekers were a series of German tourist guidebooks that the Luftwaffe used to generate targets.)

Moi and I visited York railway museum in 2013, hoping to see all six remaining Streaks together. Dominion of Canada had been loaned to York Railway museum by the Canadian government for that purpose. Mallard, Bittern, Sir Nigel Gresley, Dominion of Canada and Dwight D Eisenhower were all there, but Union of South Africa was missing. I was very disappointed. Even Moi was sympathetically disappointed also.

We'd travelled there by train with a view to making it a railway day, so after a happy few hours at the museum, we made our way back to York station, crest-fallen, dejected and deflated for not seeing all six Streaks together. But as if my magic, on the very next platform waiting to depart:

LNER (London and North East Railway) number 4488 9 60009, Union of South Africa.

This amazing coincidence made the day even more magical.

I was recently recalling the joy of comic books and model trains – which I loved as a young boy (and still do!). Another early hobby was the construction model sets I shared with my cousins the McInnes', such as Bayko Build and Meccano.

Bayko Build had a base made of Bakelite (an early form of plastic), with lots of holes to fit pins into, which held the bricks, doors and window frames, and a readymade roof would then be fitted on the top (a good place for a roof I find). The Meccano set was much more elaborate and complicated. It had brightly coloured steel bars, flat plates of various widths and lengths, pulleys and wheels of different sizes with many holes to take the small nuts and bolts that came with the set. We could make anything that our imagination could think of.

I went on to enjoy other types of construction toys when my big sis and her boyfriend (soon to become husband) John bought me an Airfix Lancaster Bomber for Christmas. I eventually constructed dozens of Airfix ships and planes. I also had the boys' favourite – the Tri-ang train set. When I was not playing outside, I would return to the Meccano set, Airfix construction kits and my Tri-ang train set many, many times throughout my childhood. All classics among toys.

One of the highlights of the year was a trip to the huge fun fair on Red Doles Lane, just off Leeds Road at the far end of Huddersfield. When I was too young to be there on my own, Mum and Dad would take me and Rhondda, and we would have a great old time on the dodgems, swings, rides and helter-skelter among many others, or the darts, hoopla and duck fishing stalls, consuming lashings of candy floss, toffee apples and brandy snaps.

We would inevitably win a goldfish in a jar, which we could only ever get to live for a few days, but the McInneses had one that lasted for many years.

At the far end of the grounds, there was a large steel construction that was shaped like a playground slide, but much bigger. I always thought it was a ride for the big boys, and it wasn't until many years later that I discovered it was part of the ready-mix concrete mixing company situated in the land next to the fairground! Moi told me recently that she also thought exactly the same thing.

As the world is changing, the land once used by the annual fair is now an industrial estate.

Boys also have more risky adventurous hobbies, all of which the more sensible women and girls find difficult to understand; many of us fellas don't understand it either, but we do it anyway and justify it by thinking we are being encouraged by the girls/ladies.

In my childhood and early youth, I was fascinated with fire. I would often throw things over the fireguard to watch them burn – usually my own toys, although I also remember throwing my leather balaclava helmet onto the fire. Even at that age, I was showing good fashion sense.

Funnily enough, I gave up throwing things on the fire when the fireguard was removed. But it didn't stop me being fascinated by other aspects of the hypnotic flame. I later found that I could squirt a constant jet of cigarette lighter fuel into the fire from the tin and control the flow so that the flame would travel back along the jet until it was just a couple of inches away from the nozzle.

My interests in fire and construction came together when I made a balsawood construction plane. Within the kit were strips and blocks of balsawood that had to be cut and glued together to a set design and then all the sections were glued together. Tissue paper was fitted to form a skin and then the whole thing was lacquered. A length of strong knicker-elastic stretched along the fuselage to a propeller at the front. It took me weeks to complete. Then it was time to try it out.

In theory, if the propeller was turned with the fingers in the correct direction the model should then fly under its own propulsion after being propelled skywards from the hand. Mine did not – it immediately came down with a thud – and extensive repairs had to be carried out. By that time, I was disappointed and fed up. When it came time for its second, less enthusiastic flight, I required extra excitement.

I wound the propeller up to full power, and in my time-honoured tradition, I set it on fire.

When I released it, I was fully expecting it to plummet instantly to the ground again, but it didn't. It flew majestically, straight and level, much better than I would have dared to hope. But by this time, things were happening that I no longer had any control over.

The lacquer, paper and balsawood were soon well alight, and nothing could be done to save it. I'm not sure that I wanted to save it anyway. None of my previous toy burning episodes came remotely close to being as impressive as that flight and I didn't burn another toy again. Not deliberately anyway.

A final fire-related episode relates to a more grown-up hobby.

During the Christmas of 1961, I was 14 years old and much more innocent and naive than 14-year-olds seem to be today. The whisky, sherry, port, black beer, and Advocaat had come out from the back of Dad's wardrobe where it had been since the previous Christmas. Mum and Dad had gone out and I decided to see what all the fuss was about with this whisky stuff.

I poured half a tumbler. Which seemed to have been the regular measure, and then took a sip. It was horrible. I wondered how anybody would drink the stuff, and I threw the remaining contents of the tumbler into the open fire.

What happened next came as a bit of a surprise. Luckily, the ensuing flash of flame didn't last more than a second, but it made me jump back so quickly that I landed on my silly arse in the middle of the room. There was no damage done.

I now find better things to do with whisky since joining the Bolster Moor Malt Whisky Appreciation Society.

Chapter 5: The Norcliffe ancestry

Many people were born, christened, married, and buried using several spellings of their name. This is true of the Norcliffe's too – Norcliffe, Nortcliffe, Northcliffe, de Northcliffe are but a few. The first half of the following is taken from ancient records, and therefore contain words and phrases that are now unfamiliar and that I've tried to translate.

Historical records of the family

The following is an extract from the history of prominent local families found in the Dodsworth manuscripts in the Bodleian Library at Oxford.

From the early times in Norcliffe, there have existed three dwellings – Upper Norcliffe, (Norcliffe Hall), Lower Norcliffe, and Little Norcliffe. The site gave its name to a family and there are indications of this in ancient local records.

Among the Dodsworth manuscripts in the Bodleian Library at Oxford, is a pedigree compiled from notes made by John Hanson of Rastrick, our 17th century antiquary. This pedigree is authenticated by extracts from the early deeds. It gives evidence of the Northcliffe's dating back to at least the 13th century.

It begins with John of Northcliffe. Agnes of Cromwell Bottom, in the days of her widowhood, granted John's son Thomas, and his heirs, 35 acres of land in Northcliffe.

According to the pedigree, Thomas had a son called Henry. Evidence from the Wakefield court rolls shows that Henry of Norcliffe took lands off the Lord of the manor of Wakefield in

1309, as a freeman holding land in Hipperholme.

The Richard of Norcliffe enigma

Henry was succeeded by his son Richard. One of the Dodsworth deeds confirms that in 1332, Richard gave "to John son of John of Owram and to Alice his wife and the heirs of their bodies" all his land and tenement in Southowram, Hipperholme.

This is rather an enigma, because in the same year (1332), Richard conveyed two acres of "copyhold" in Hipperholme to "John of Norcliffe".

Richard left only three daughters and no son to inherit the estate. The first of these daughters married a Rookes, of the Rookes of Hipperholme. The second, Matilda, didn't marry. The third, Emmota, married Adam of Hopton.

When Richard of Norcliffe died, probably shortly after 1375, the estate was divided into three portions among his daughters. Two of these portions remained in the hands of the Rookes family until the 16th century, one share, according to the compiler of notes, came to that family by marriage.

This is hard to reconcile with the fact that in 1540, one-third part was still owned by a member of the Norcliffe family, and this part was apparently the portion known as Little Norcliffe.

This is the enigma. How, if Richard left only three daughters as his heiresses, did one-third part remain in the possession of a family that bore the good old local name? Is it possible that John Norcliffe, who inherited the Hipperholme estates from Richard, married his cousin Matilda, the daughter and co-heiress whose husband's name is not known by Dodsworth?

An old deed preserved in the monument room at Langton Hall – the present seat of the descendants of the Norcliffe's – shows that John Norcliffe of Barsland "granted to Thomas Gledhill of Barsland and others for a term of years, a rent of 35/4 issuing out all lands and tenements called 'The Norcliffe Tercia'".

This branch of the Norcliffe family seem to have settled in Barkisland. I've not yet been able to discover to whom or when these Norcliffe's of Barkisland sold Little Norcliffe, with the acres from which the family traced their name. In 1582, Thomas and his wife Elizabeth sold two messuages (an old term meaning dwelling house with outbuildings and land assigned to its use) in Barkisland, and moved to Gomersal where he purchased an estate in the same year.

In Burkes Landed Gentry, the pedigree of Norcliffe of Langton is traced up to Nicholas, the father of John Norcliffe of Barkisland, named in the deed of 1540 relating to Little Norcliffe.

John had a son Stephen, whose son was Thomas originally of Barkisland. He was buried at Nunnington in 1616.The grant of arms, made to him by the heralds, is still preserved among the family papers. He married Elizabeth, daughter of Robert Ealand Carlinghow, and had a son, Sir Thomas Norcliffe, Knight Barrister of the middle temple, High Sheriff for Yorkshire 1626, who purchased Langton, County York 1618.

As we see, Sir Thomas Norcliffe moved to Langton Hall, near Malton in North Yorkshire In 1618. Still in God's country I was glad to learn. However, it is where my Barkisland line and the Norcliffe's of Langton diverge.

The Langton Norcliffes.

Langton is a very pleasant little village with a small but beautifully proportioned church. Both the village and church show much evidence that the Norcliffes had some influence there. How things have changed, I struggle to achieve any influence in my own home.

Several examples of family connections within the Norcliffe Coat of Arms over Langton church exit.

As was the fashion in those days when a gentleman from one relatively powerful family was betrothed to a lady from a much more powerful family, particularly a family from the landed gentry with a seat and arms, then the gentleman would be obliged to take the family name of his wife. He could only take the seat and arms if he agreed to do so. This was the case when Thomas inherited Langton, he was obliged to take the name and arms of Norcliffe through marrying into the family and estate. Thomas had previously been known as Dalton (eldest son of John Dalton by Isabella, daughter of Sir John Wray baronet). Thomas joined the army and obtained a troop in the 11th Dragoons, and was lieutenant colonel of the York Volunteers for 29 years. He married Ann in 1784 and they had six children: Norcliffe (who died aged five), William (who died at 15), Thomas, Isabella, Charlotte and Mary.

This system of marrying off eligible daughters and sons within the landed gentry ensured that the wealth, land, money and power stayed within the ruling classes, and woe betide any love-struck individuals who dared to rock the boat and attempt to marry anyone outside their class boundaries. They would very likely run the risk of being disinherited without a penny. Best take a lover after a decent period following a proper marriage would probably be the advice. I'm not sure if this system and advice isn't still being encouraged.

The son of Thomas and his wife Isabella was named Thomas Norcliffe Norcliffe 1791-1862, who became Major General Sir Norcliffe Norcliffe, portrait wearing his uniform from when he was a colonel is shown overleaf. Many high ranking offices bought their commission, there is some evidence that some continued to buy further commissions after they retired from military service. This Thomas in turn had a daughter also named Isabella, and this Isabella, was a close friend and possible partner for a time of Anne Lister, of Shibden Hall, Halifax, Anne was known locally as 'Gentleman Jack' due to her sexuality, (batting for the other side). Shibden Hall to Langton Hall is about 65 miles – in a coach and horses that's quite a journey, even with a posh coach! They must have been quite keen on each other. Incidentally, the theme song to the BBC series "Gentleman Jack" was performed by O'Hooley and Tidow of Golcar. And very nice it is too.

My direct family tree goes back to 1210 to a John de Northcliffe of Barsland (now Barkisland). They were influential landowners and two were high sheriffs of Yorkshire. When Thomas inherited Langton Hall in 1618, it left the rest of us riff raff with all their Norcliffe land in Barkisland to fend for ourselves.

*This is the portrait of my distant cousin, Major General Sir Norcliffe Norcliffe, of Langton. 1791–1862.
18th Kings Irish Regiment of Light Dragoons (Hussars).*

I'm sure he wouldn't claim me as his distant cousin.

This was the portrait that provoked uncontrollable swooning from our very own Colonel of the W.A.R.T.S. described in a previous ramble.

Like many of the Gentry, the Langton Norcliffes carried on the tradition of 'primogeniture' whereby the eldest son inherits his parents' entire estate, and the younger sons take a commission in the military or join the clergy. Many Norcliffes achieved high ranks in the army.

Incidentally, none of the Norcliffe land, title or estate has come my way, not even the second-best bed!

Chapter 7: How the other half lives, or at least try to live

My experiences during my work as a technical officer within a council housing grant system, and while I was a building clerk of works for a local city property service department, certainly showed me how very much better off I was than many. People with nothing have no idea how the rich manage to spend their millions, and the rich have no idea how people get by on tuppence, and I'm sure don't want to know either. Some of the homes I visited showed what poverty and deprivation really looks like.

Several of the homes I would visit had filthy half-naked children running about in filthy rooms where the carpet was covered with rubbish and all too often animal excrement. Invariably, the parent would be crashed out on something, and I wouldn't be able to get a coherent conversation.

Contractors are a very hardy bunch, and are prepared to work in conditions where others would never tread. This means they are often the first to identify extreme poverty and take the necessary steps to get help for the people concerned.

I recall one team of contractors asking me to check out a property, with a view to getting the tenants some sort of help, or perhaps moved into better accommodation or social care.

Signs of deprivation and poverty are usually visible from the outside of a house. These can feel like signs of impending doom as you approach the door. Rough, unkempt gardens with rubbish strewn everywhere, curtains closed … or, as in this case, an old blanket fastened to the inside of the lounge window.

I knocked on the door and an elderly gentleman opened it. I was immediately hit by the overwhelming smell. He had obviously not been in contact with soap for some time, or indeed a comb, razor or barber. He was wearing a paisley shirt and woollen trousers but they had been worn for so long that they had taken on a leather look.

On entering the lounge we found an elderly lady sat on the couch. She had no legs and was confused and upset that we were there. Between the couch and the fireplace were two buckets that were used as toilets; one was full the other half full. It was very difficult to breath in the pungent atmosphere.

I was in no doubt that the couple were in desperate need of help, and I referred the case to the council care department. They were soon moved out into a setting where they could be properly looked after. During the time when councils felt that they could afford rent collectors that knocked on the door, these problems would have been identified, but the world of 'direct debit and standing orders' means that the council officials rarely see their tenants nor their housing stock.

During my earlier work for the government private housing grant schemes, assessments for eligibility had to be carried out. For a grant to be successful, it had to include details of all the improvements needed in the house to bring it up to a decent living standard, which was where I came in. I therefore had to inspect every room in a property.

I visited a house on one occasion and a woman answered the door. As I entered and went into the lounge/dining/kitchen area, I noticed a huge, overweight German Shepherd dog that was finding it difficult to move about. There were empty, licked clean plates all over the floor, and the sink was piled high with many more licked clean plates and crockery. It looked as though very little traditional washing up was done, and instead the house-holder just kept buying new plates. The dog obviously enjoyed all the leftovers.

Eventually I entered the master bedroom. As was often the case, the lights wouldn't work, and once again there was a blanket fastened to the window. I stepped inside and waited for my eyes to become accustomed to the darkness, and to my shock I noticed a pair of grubby, decaying feet sticking out from under the bed covers.

I looked for some signs of life, but for all the world it appeared to be a body with a sheet covering it entirely except the feet. I stood there for ages hoping for some sort of happy outcome, but suspecting the worse. Eventually, and to my great relief, a man finally turned over with a groan. I never did see any other part of his body, I'm glad to say, nor did we enter into any sort of conversation.

The small adjoining bedroom that contained a pair of bunk beds had a rope fastened between the door handle and the banister rail so that the door could be tied shut. This case also went to a higher authority.

I visited another house that was occupied by a man who was in hospital at the time. Before he was released back to his home, I had to inspect the house to assess it for safety and partly for his needs during recovery.

What we found was a house stacked with stuff from floor to ceiling. A very narrow passageway led from the front door, to the kitchen, downstairs toilet and lounge chair where he slept. There were piles and piles of papers and boxes.

We couldn't get upstairs, but from the back garden we could see that the rear bedroom window was missing. Not just a glass pane – the whole window frame was resting among the brambles in the garden. The garden was so overgrown that the greenhouse was buried up to the very tip. I learned from the NHS officials that the occupant was a landscape gardener. It must have been awful for him to have allowed the house and garden to decay to that extent.

He never did return to his home, his family decided that he was better off in residential care. It might have been nice if they'd visited from time to time before it reached that point. But perhaps they did, and I'm being unkind. It's possible he simply refused help until his health became so bad that the family could make the decision for him, which is often the case.

Many people slip through the net for all sorts of reasons. As a society, and as families, it is up to us to make sure we love and care for all our people, no matter how great or small to prevent poverty and deprivation.

Chapter 7: Musical Performances

Singing was very popular in our local churches, chapels and schools. Mum had always been very musical. She joined her Knowl Bank school choir in 1927, when she was eight years old.

Mum's dad, Edward, was an amateur choirmaster and organist for two Golcar chapels. Mum's first memory of music was while walking down a country lane with her dad and he broke into singing Wagner's "Hail Bright Abode". He had a wonderful bass voice. In 1921, Mum's Knowl Bank school choir competed in the school choir section at the very prestigious Llangollen Eisteddfod competition and won.

My grandfather also encouraged me to sing – solos for family gatherings – as he had with his own children when they were young. At primary school, I joined (was press-ganged) into the Golcar Church school choir. We competed in the Huddersfield Mrs Sunderland competition in 1958 and came sixth out of 12. We were very pleased with our modest position, as we were the only junior school competing.

I did nothing with any music talent that I may, or may not, have inherited for a few years, until sometime around 1959, when my brother-in-law John gave me an acoustic guitar. To begin with, I just jammed with friends and played for an occasional more organised singsong and birthday parties. Then eventually, along with the aforementioned John, we instigated the re-birth of the band 'Antique Gold'.

Re-birth of "Antique Gold" for John's, on the left, 65th Birthday 2006.
For the sad amongst us, the guitars are Fender, Les Paul and Burns.

My choir commitment began again in 1990, when an old work colleague, Albert Collins, persuaded me to join Gledholt Male Voice Choir. Albert was one of the world's lovely fellas. He was an ex-scrum half for Keighley Rugby League, and he was also my first rugby league coach.

Gledholt Choir were very welcoming, all very friendly. I have, or at least had, a natural baritone voice, but as I could reach bottom D and could manage two-and-a-bit octaves, from bottom D to top F – an acceptable bass range – I was placed in the bass section alongside David Porter.

David became my mentor and even though we have both moved on he continues to be a very good friend.

We left Gledholt and then both joined the Colne Valley male voice choir, which was a much better choir, with many fantastic singers. The choirmaster, Thom Meredith, and the accompanist, Keith Swallow, are very accomplished musicians and second to none.

Colne Valley MVC has always been a competition choir, competing in and winning many, including the Llangollen Eisteddfod six times. If the pressure wasn't enough already, in the 1999 competition, Thom had us standing with voice parts mixed up, such that we could only stand next to one other in our own section.

Luckily my mate David and I sang together which helped me stay in tune, as David is an excellent harmoniser. If singing mixed doesn't teach harmonising nothing will. The mixing paid off as that was one we won.

In 1998 we also won first prize at the Pontrhyfendigaid Eisteddfod, (try saying that with a mouth full of crackers) in May, and we again achieved first at Llangollen in July, and first at the National Male Voice Choir Championship at Rhyl in October. Colne Valley MVC thus became the only Choir to accomplish the superb double of the Male Voice Choir of the World and the National Male Voice Choir Champions in the same year.

Also in 1999, was yet another highlight, as we sang in Rouen Cathedral and mass at Reims Cathedral, the mass being sung in French. The only unfortunate coincidence of this tour was that we were staying in a hotel in Rouen for a few nights, including 30 May. To the uninitiated – and I was one, as were the tour organisers – this was the place and date of the execution of Joan of Arc in 1431. We did wonder for a while why we weren't too popular. 568 years is a long time to hold a grudge init.

Just to show off, we also sang Pilgrim's Chorus in German that year. All our singing was performed without music on stage;

Thom Meredith the musical director liked to keep our minds boiling over.

I joined several full and sub committees, one of which was the Yorkshire Cancer Research Festival Committee. This was initially to organise the 1,000 Yorkshire male voices event, which took place every four years at the Royal Albert Hall, London. During the run-up to the 2003 concert, it was decided to invite ladies' choirs also. I was asked to be stage manager, and I foolishly agreed, not knowing what I was in for. (As David has often said "If you want a volunteer, ask a busy man".)

Eventually I had to find 1,500 choir places, all demanding that they sit within their section. Therefore, I had to ascertain how many from eight sections, each of the 20 choirs were sending, add them up and section off within the Albert Hall stage maps, the number of seats I required and where.

Luckily, I was provided with several maps by Mo, the Albert Hall's very helpful manager. However, Sid, the committee chairman was determined to sell every ticket and every space.

Each meeting he would tell me he had sold more tickets and eventually the audience seating encroached onto the seats I had been allocated for the choirs. This happened four times and each time I had to rearrange the choir seating on the map, meticulously colouring each group of seats for each section.

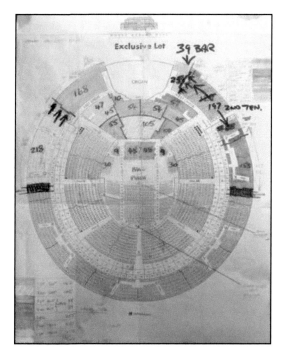

The fourth and final seating plan, though even this
had some last-minute adjustments (in black).
A nightmare. I was always good at colouring-in though, a natural.

During the Friday before the concert in our hotel bed, I woke up in the night in a cold sweat, knowing I hadn't enough seats. Luckily Mo came to the rescue again, and during the morning rehearsal her staff scoured every corner of the building and found seats in the repair shop or used by the maintenance staff until I had just enough, with not one to spare.

The audience had been pushed in from the sides, and so the choir was squashed in and down into the space that the two brass bands were occupying. These were in turn pushed further forward until the knees of the band were almost touching the knees of the audience. One chap on the front row said to me that the slide from the trombone player was flashing past his ear hole! An exaggeration of course, but it can't have been far from the truth.

For all of that, we all had a great time. As happened on many occasions after a concert, the choirs would find a bar somewhere and start singing again. In this case many bars!

Before the start of the concert, I found myself backstage in the wrong place at the wrong time. As I was the only one in the festival office at that moment wearing a black tie and dress suit, I was asked to announce arrangements for a section of the audience after the concert.

Norky speaking to a 5,000 audience in the Albert Hall.

It isn't a very good photo, but this is me speaking to five thousand people in the Albert Hall just before the two bands took the stage. Everybody was so thrilled to be there that I received rapturous applause for announcing coach pickup points. On leaving the stage, Norman, the soloist and fellow committee member said, "Bloody hell Peter, it'll be a bugger if my applause isn't as good as that". It was of course… just.

Some Yorkshire humour;

A Yorkshire man visits the vet's.

"Nah-then vetenry, mi cat goes aht evry neet an int mornin' it's staggrin' abaht on wobbly legs then sleeps all t' day, thanose".

The vet asks "It's a tom I assume"

"Nay lad, I've brung it wi me".

While my wife Moi was working in medical admin, a patient rang to ask for an appointment. The surgery receptionist asked her for a brief description of the condition and the patient said, "I've got this eer itchin'". The receptionist quite understandably wrote down in the appointment book "Itching ear".

When the doctor eventually saw the patient, it turned out the itching was in another part of the body entirely. I suspect they were both surprised when she dropped her drawers and the doctor took out his otoscope.

Artwork by Stan

Chapter 8: Slowly becoming more civilised

Norky riding for The White Knights
on 'Concrete' an ex police Honda ST 1100 Pan European.

The young do many things that would seem to be inappropriate. In my experience, boys are predominately the most guilty. I am somewhat of an expert in these matters as I've been a boy for over 74 years. Remembering back to my childhood and I now think, "Why did I do that?" Terrible twos, tantrum threes, flaysome (frightening) fours, fearsome fives and it goes on!

During one of my big sister's playful moments, she told me that mum had seriously considered an abortion, but the doctor said that seeing as I had already started school, it's a little late.

I won't describe some of the things that I experimented with at around that age, safe to say that no one came to any harm. But if an adult had discovered what I was experimenting with, I'm sure there would have been concerns about my menace to society. Luckily I eventually grew out of it and slowly began to be civilised. That is until I became 16.

Many young boys do things that are antisocial and definitely inappropriate. If caught, the child is then made to feel guilty and steps are put in place to stop them doing it again. In my humble opinion, this often stops the child's natural development into knowing right from wrong. I stress that even though others were sometimes involved, if anyone was hurt by my experiments, it was me.

There are many arguments on whether our personality is dictated by nature or nurture, and whether people are naturally evil or sociopathic. I cannot answer how these things develop, but I do know that many children, including myself, can be cruel and antisocial, but thankfully grow up to be almost civilised. Some of this obnoxious behaviour returns during puberty, as it did with me.

As a teenager, I had a great time with my many biking mates, but we were definitely laddish, and no doubt seemed threatening as a group. I can assure our readers that as far as I'm aware, no animals were deliberately harmed during the period of our combined puberty and youth.

I never liked how the police were magically always around when I wanted to have fun during my early biking days. They made attempts to stop me doing it and I quickly resented their presence. I wasn't good with any type of authority really – my bosses were always wrong, which didn't do my job prospects much good. What I'm trying to describe in my clumsy way, is that foolish boys can eventually begin to see the error of their way.

I eventually realised that good driving isn't fast driving, but safe driving. As this realisation dawned, I took an advanced driving course in first motorcycle and then car, eventually becoming an observer for motorcycle. An observer in the Institute of Advanced Motorists (IAM) is someone who helps trainee members through their IAM training. I also used this advanced skill as a rider and eventually Huddersfield manager of the blood product delivery system White Knights.

White Knights are a voluntary, out-of-hours blood products delivery service. At the time I was riding for them, we used former police bikes.

The photo is me on a Honda ST 1100 Pan European; very nice bikes. All our bikes retained their police call signs, and this particular bike was called 'Concrete' because when it was a police bike the rider rode it into a newly laid patch of concrete and managed to get it stuck. I know this is true because the sad photo is in the White Knights' records, and no doubt it was pinned to the responsible officer's locker, I can just imagine what abuse he got for that one.

We deliberately took on the appearance of police officers to be able to get through the traffic quickly, and Concrete still had its blue lights working so I used them during my urgent runs, perhaps I shouldn't have, but I did, and I have to say, it was tremendous fun, and compensated for all the runs I did through the night.

To show how much we can grow up if given the chance, I even forgave the police for their earlier transgressions into spoiling my fun and I became a community volunteer, working exclusively with the police during event marshalling and public advice stalls and targeted area leaflet deliveries.

Marshalling in Holmfirth during the Tour de France in 2014 was a fantastic experience. Thousands of spectators turned out. I had no idea that there was so much support and security involved. There were many British police outriders, on their Bayerrische Motoren Werke AG (BMW) motorcycles. All seemed to be entering into the spirit by high-fiving the spectators as they rode past.

The British police on their blue, white and yellow BMW's, and the French police on their blue Yamaha's.

Perhaps they took the opportunity to smack the heads of a couple of those they recognised, but I didn't witness anything like that; they all seemed to be having fun. The French police on their blue Yamaha bikes, on the other hand seemed a bit grumpy – no high-fiving from them. Perhaps they knew that they wouldn't recognise anyone in Yorkshire to smack.

I also helped on the police information stall at the Honley country show 2014. I had done this sort of work several times and it's always amusing how the public react to seeing the police when they don't expect it. Most people are very friendly of course and will stop for a chat. Some amusingly will quickly and obviously avert their gaze and rush past.

Given a chance, most people will grow up; boys just seem to take a little longer. It appears that when we become very old and our brain turns to mush, we regress back to our childhood. If this happens to me, I don't envy whoever has to change my nappy, particularly if I'm not fed. I know I'll be a very grumpy old git, there are signs that it's happening already, but so far I'm okay with my own nappy changing.

Chapter 9: Medical interventions

In 1986, Moi and I decided that we'd all the children we wanted and by that time Moira had been on the birth control pill for over ten years. We thought that was long enough, so Moira proposed a vasectomy as the best option. When I agreed to this, I hadn't realised it would have to be me who would be subjected to the knife; I'm sure an anatomy lecture would have covered this subject, but I must have been absent that day.

I agree that it's a big decision to make for any man, but the alternative is for the woman to run the risk of pregnancy (by continuing with less-reliable options), or for her to have her tubes tied, both being potentially dangerous.

My particular vasectomy operation and aftermath were very straightforward; the only interesting aspect was the sense of humour shown by the surgeon. Geoffrey Bunch was a very capable general surgeon in the Huddersfield area. Within his repertoire he carried out many vasectomies, including mine.

Mr Bunch would tell many amusing stories around the dinner table at the Colne Valley Choir functions, of which he was chair and later president. After his retirement he would do the same when he was acting as a speaker at various functions. Mr Bunch was a witty man with a dry sense of humour. I've painted this picture in order to show how he would like to brighten the day of his operating room staff, if not necessarily brighten the day of the patient on the table.

Mr Bunch carried out his vasectomies in the operating theatre at St Luke's Hospital. For my big day, I'd opted for a local anaesthetic, which was unusual for the time. I was wheeled into the theatre, under the hot glare of the overhead lights. Mr Bunch then proceeded to cover my body with the hot green covers straight from the sterilising oven, exposing only the offending area and my head (some may say both are offending).

I was trying to look cool and in control, I was also trying to take interest in what was happening around the parts that were, after all, the centre of the universe to me. But I was getting hotter and hotter. I asked a nurse if she could get me a cold cloth for my forehead, as I was still trying to take some interest.

We got to a stage where I assumed things were going to start happening. At that point, Mr Bunch nonchalantly waved a huge pair of grippy, crampy things in front of my face. They had long handles with snarly teeth at the other end. I thought, "What the hell is he going to do with them?" In fact, he used them to clamp the edges of the green covers together! Obviously, what he wanted was for me to put my head back and to keep quiet and it certainly did the trick.

Another entertaining episode occurred during a small operation I'd had a few years earlier. The operation was to remove a piece of wire that had become lodged through a guider and into a knuckle of my right hand. It wasn't a serious injury, but the surgeon suggested a full anaesthetic as the safer option, as any movement on my part during its removal could be catastrophic for that hand.

I dutifully attended the day patient clinic and was fitted with the classic knee-length theatre gown of the type that are guaranteed to give people a good laugh from the back, as they expose the wearer's bare bottom. These things are not designed for walking about with any dignity, but this was not going to be the only laugh for the staff this day. The normal procedure was that the day care ward's trolleys and the theatre trolleys were kept separate, the patient would be transferred to the appropriate trolley at the entrance to and from the theatre.

After the operation, as I was being transferred to the day care trolley I started to regain consciousness, I looked down to witness the theatre sheet being drawn back to reveal that my gown was up around my chest and in my left hand I was proudly displaying a magnificent … er … erection (the best I could manage anyway). Luckily, I was conscious enough to recognise it as being my own hand and my own erection. I'm not sure if that makes it any better.

Anyway, in my anaesthetic stupor I couldn't work out why it was there or what was happening, and did nothing to cover it up. It seems that during the operation, I became very pleased to make someone's acquaintance, and the theatre staff thought that they would have another laugh. I'm sure Mr. Bunch would have left to something more important by then.

I could just imagine the nurses gathered around the bar room table that evening comparing notes about all the embarrassed patients they had seen that day, like Norcliffe-of-Scapegoat-Hill and his excitable wedding tackle. "Naughty boy"

I'm sure you will be glad to learn that there are no images connected with my medical interventions episode.

However, as a distraction, I thought I would add some random images from our walks around Huddersfield and Todmorden.

From left to right. 121, foot Stoodley Pike monument overlooking Todmorden, erected in 1815, to celebrate kicking Napoleon's arse.

The second is not a chimney, never was, and never will be. It is in fact a bat tower, yes, a tower for bats. It is 20 feet tall, was erected in 1999, at a cost of £15,000. It is on the Colne Valley circular walk, but hidden behind an old mill. It was erected with the collaboration of The Colne Valley Project, and the West Yorkshire Bat Group. Mmmmm, takes all sorts I suppose.

The third is Castle Hill monument overlooking Huddersfield, erected on a 4,000 year old settlement. This Victoria tower was completed in 1899, and is often referred to as The Jubilee Tower as it celebrated Queen Victoria's diamond jubilee two years earlier.

Chapter 10: Accidents happen

Battered helmet and goggles,
the result of the only time I came-off with a pillion passenger
which happened to be Moi about a month after our marriage.

Like many young people, I thought that I was quickly running into the 'fast forward' period where I wouldn't have much time before the dreaded adulthood and old fart period set in, forever and ever. Little did we all know that adulthood is simply what we make of it and can be just as much fun as our youth but with more security and without the interest of the police. This security of age is just a part of 'growing up'.

I had many bike accidents. When I was late picking Moi up she knew that I'd come-off or had been run in by the police. Funnily enough, my worst road traffic accident wasn't on a bike, it occurred in February 1965, when I was 17 years old. I was with a biking mate, Dooley, in an Austin A35 van owned and driven by one of Dave's mates Brad. As there were no seats in the back of the van, I had to just wedge myself behind the front seats as best I could.

We set off on that cold February evening for some Manchester night-life entertainment, travelling over the Isle of Sky Road down towards Lancashire, Brad misjudged a double bend. Truth is, he was racing another car driven by a friend of his that we had met on the way.

If anyone would consider taking up any form of racing, an Austin A35 van would never be your first choice, in fact, it wouldn't be on the list at all. However, Brad just couldn't resist the challenge. We got into a spin and hit a wall with the offside of the van travelling backwards, I was slung out of the back doors and the van probably ran over me while it continued its spin down the road. I regained consciousness a few minutes later. I remember laying on my back with my legs up the wall that we had just met. I also remember being bathed in a warm, comfortable silence until the second that I realised that there was something very wrong, then I was hit by a mountain of pain. It was like every nerve ending from my hips up was switched on.

In the meantime the van had come to a stop with its one remaining headlight shining towards where it had come from. There were no seat belts in those days, and Dooley found himself in the driver's seat, and Brad was somehow sat on the steering wheel and draped over Dooley's shoulder. They could see everything that was once in the back of the van scattered across the road, the spare wheel and my helmet (I should have been wearing it) were still rolling to a stop, but as yet no sign of me.

By this time I had managed to get into a foetal position on my hands a knees, still desperately trying to find some oxygen from the air. Just then the others arrived and tried to help but I didn't want anybody to touch me, adrenaline was beginning to kick in and I managed to gasp "leave me alone, I'll be alright in a minute", but I wasn't of course. I was taken to Oldham Hospital and with help I was able to walk into casualty. But that was the last walking I did for four days.

In my humble opinion and experience, the motionlessness foetal position is the default position that we adopt if we are badly hurt but conscious, not the demented rolling about like a half chopped worm that the kickerball players seem to adopt.

I woke up in the middle of the first night at Oldham hospital busting for a pee, the nurses had thoughtfully left a bottle at the side of the bed, but I couldn't move anything from the waist up. I was too embarrassed to ask for help of course, so it took me one and a half hours to reach and use that bottle. My bladder had expanded to the size of a bucket and I overflowed the bottle, but good grief, I don't think I had ever felt so relieved during my previous 17 years. Except perhaps when I was marooned in a Blackpool police station for hours after I got lost when I was six years old, that also resulted in my bladder taking on the dimensions of a bucket.

A couple of student nurses would make regular visits to make me welcome and listen to my funny accent. And a couple of grown up nurses – who reminded me of a very popular television program called *Emergency Ward 10* – occasionally held my hand during the first night when I wasn't feeling at my best. It almost made the whole episode worthwhile.

I received quite a lot of kudos and interest within the biking group after that. It would have been much better had I received the injuries while falling from a motorcycle, but I would soon be adding many other stories of heroic survival of the most breath-taking bike accidents when I cheated death only by inches. All true, if not just a *little* exaggerated.

Four days down the line they decided to take quite a number of x-rays. Amongst many lacerations, concussion, missing lumps and bruises, the X-rays showed I'd broken my right elbow. The staff asked me why I hadn't told them that my arm hurt, my telling them that I couldn't tell which bit hurt the most didn't seem to satisfy them much.

The next day, the orthopaedic consultant recommended a straight plaster cast. My arm was bent at the time and I found it very painful to move it at all. When it was time for the orthopaedic technician to straighten my arm, they must have assumed that it (or me) would prove troublesome, and the resident gorilla was on standby at the back of the room in case I kicked up a rumpus. Luckily, if I relaxed and allowed the very nice and sympathetic technician to move my arm, there was very little pain and the gorilla was not required, much to the relief of the technician who I think was more than a little concerned.

I left Oldham Hospital after a few days, and attended Huddersfield Royal Infirmary for the remaining treatment. The resident orthopaedic consultant there wasn't impressed with the straight cast idea and recommended fitting a bent cast this time. Again, another local gorilla was on standby just in case. But as before this wasn't necessary and he was sent chuntering on his way. I have to say, whether it was the straight or bent cast, or even a combination of both, it seemed to have worked, for I have not had a minutes bother with that arm/elbow following the returned muscle strength a few weeks later.

I found that the bent cast was much more practical. And after I accidentally softened the bent section in the bath, I was even able to ride my bike again! I had to change my riding style a little and I couldn't shift my weight around or stick my knee out quite as far as before, but I managed.

I'd copied this style from a bike racing hero of mine called John Cooper (Mooneyes, hence the eyes on my own helmet). I seem to remember he was the first rider to develop a style where he would lean his body off the bike into the bends and stick his leg out and on occasion slide his knee along the tarmac. This is the style now used by all racing motorcyclists, and all riders who think they are. Before Mooneyes, all riders sat squarely on the bike through the bends.

As I'm right handed, having a plaster cast on my right arm made many things awkward or impossible, but being 17 years old and 'immortal' I soon adjusted. I often got the sympathy vote from the young women and I was even able to continue playing darts quite well with my left hand. The two things that I was never able to quite get to grips with were combing my hair and wiping my arse.

Luckily I recovered quickly, and after six weeks the cast was removed and I was near to full recovery. But I had a skinny, hairy right arm to build back up again and my neck took a couple of years to feel completely comfortable. Even after more than 55 years, I still get a twinge in my back that corresponds to the area of a tear in my suit jacket.

Brad's father offered to pay for the repairs to my suit. No offer of a replacement or any other compensation, and Brad's insurance wouldn't pay out either (apparently Brad didn't pay for insurance that covered his passengers). I could have sued his ass and I probably should have, but loyalty has always meant a great deal to me.

Chapter 11: The Wakefield Bierkeller beginning of another adventure

When Moira feels the need to describe what a proper git I have been she relates an incident that happened soon after Rachel was born, 1969/70. I always point out that I was a completely innocent party to other people's recklessness. I should also point out that Moi is never persuaded by this excuse. If the city of Wakefield is ever mentioned, it's never long before Moi says, "that reminds me"

This was actually in Huddersfield Bierkeller in about 1975, but it was very similar to the Wakefield Bierkeller at the time.

More happy days.

During a visit from an old biking mate called Dave Hill (Pill), who had previously moved to Canada, he suggested that the lads could get together and visit the Wakefield Bierkeller. Bierkellers were fashionable at the time, because; lager was served in one-litre steins and the furniture included very simple long benches and tough trestle tables, on which everyone was encouraged to dance. The fashion didn't last long but was fun all the same.

I'd been taken in the car belonging to John (Rubber Duck) along with Paul who happens to be the W.A.R.T.S. chief engineer, and the late David Coop (Coot), one of life's lovely fellas.

Pill had hired an MG Roadster sports car in the hope that it would impress everyone, and his passenger was Colin (Crabby).

Crabby and Pill alongside the MG Roadster 1967/68.

We had been having a good time throughout the evening and when it came time to leave we were unaware that there had been some trouble outside and the police were still milling about, one of whom was a dog handler.

Coot, Paul, Rubber Duck and I were strolling towards the car when Rubber Duck decided to give the dog handler some verbal abuse. This came as a big surprise, as Rubber Duck was never usually like that. Within minutes, the police officer had him pinned up against a shop window while trying to keep the dog from separating Rubber Duck from his vitals. We were trying to placate the situation but the officer's colleagues made sure we couldn't get close. Our friend was taken to the nearby police station.

Rubber Duck is quite tall and the police dog handler was very short (for a police officer). I will always be amused by the image of the police officer frogmarching Rubber Duck down the road while lifting him onto his tiptoes by his jacket collar, still holding his dog in the other hand while it continued trying to chew on some part of Rubber Duck's anatomy and making a hell of a racket, the dog that is, although Rubber Duck was making a bit of a whimpering noise of his own.

We followed at a discrete distance and asked the desk sergeant if we could have our friend back. He said that John was in for the night. When we asked for the car keys, the request was impolitely declined. We were told to "go away". Well, I think it was something like that.

At the railway station, we discovered there were no trains to Huddersfield. Our combined pool of money wasn't enough for a taxi either. So we decided we had no alternative but to walk the 18 miles home.

Unbeknownst to us, while we were investigating our options at the railway station, the police had released Rubber Duck, who'd returned to his car and tried to find us but never thought to look at railway station. He assumed we'd been picked up by some other mates and he drove back towards Huddersfield.

In the meantime Pill, with his passenger Crabby, had an accident while entering the main road onto Huddersfield. Apparently, he was still driving in Canada and looked the wrong way.

There were no serious injuries, but Pill knew he'd been drinking and could be in serious trouble, so he pretended to be hurt, at which point Rubber Duck appeared on the scene, freshly released from the police cells. Arrangements were made to take Pill and Crabby to hospital in Rubber Duck's car, in the hope that this would waste enough time for Pill to sober up.

Coot, Paul and I were merrily oblivious to all this and we were still striding out manfully when, several hours later (approximately four-o-clock in the morning), Rubber Duck drove past my house on his way home from the hospital and noticed a light on. He knocked on the door to make sure I was okay.

Moira answered and said, "Where is he?" Rubber Duck, in his infinite wisdom, assumed she meant Pill, and assumed that she already knew about the accident; and knowing that Moi didn't like Pill, he worked all this out in a split second and said "he's dead". When Moi tells this story there is always a little crescendo just there.

Luckily, Rubber Duck soon realised that he'd said the wrong thing and belatedly checked to see whether I was home. Moi said, "Well, as a matter of fact, you may be surprised to learn that he is not", or words to that effect. He told Moi the fuller story as he knew it, and quickly vacated the area. I was still half an hour away and merrily oblivious.

I've never been allowed to forget it, not that I really want to forget. It's an amusing story that's provided many, many, hours of family entertainment and I still maintain that I was a completely innocent party to the whole episode.

Chapter 12: Lovely ladies

Moira Hirst in 1965. I was like lamb to the slaughter.

These were days of ignorance and innocence that many young people of today would find surprising. We knew nothing about sex and we were expected to fumble our way through puberty and adolescence hoping things work out well. The risk of pregnancy was our main form of birth control. I knew one person who was using the contraceptive pill as early as 1963, just three years after the pill was first introduced in the states. For a lady to admit that they took the initiative in birth control was very unusual, even if she was married or in a steady relationship. She would have easily been regarded as a brazen hussy, therefore, many ladies didn't admit to taking any initiative at all. "Just lay back and think of England" was the earlier official advice and hope that the man knew what he was doing. But we didn't know what we were doing. In many ways, that was part of the fun, risk and excitement. We were still expected to find a partner, get married after a reasonable engagement period and have a child within a couple of years. It had been normal from the beginning of time that an intimate relationship resulted in pregnancy. That's how things had gone on, or variations of the same for thousands of years; at some point a man and woman formed a relationship that best ensured the survival of the offspring.

Because of the maturity of a human child, it is unable to look after itself for ten years or more, therefore the father needed to stay around for at least that long, to provide for the mother and his offspring, which inevitably resulted in more children, and marriage of some sort was a convenient and natural development. It appears that children are not able to look after themselves for 30 years or more now.

Modern children take several generations to achieve some sort of maturity, hiding in their parents or grandparents back bedrooms until they decide to venture out into the bad, bad world and cure all its ails in one go, and it comes as a big shock that the world is as bad as it is, and they find that they have to shout a lot. I look forward to the time when they retreat to mummy's back bedroom again, and keep quiet until they grow up. I don't think I will ever get used to the young. I have developed an almost constant grumble about them. I'm sure past generations had the same attitude. I know my parent's generation did. Even the wimpy millennial snowflakes are complaining about us Baby Boomers, but of course they were/are all jealous that the baby boomers had the best of everything. They benefited from the newly formed welfare state, the National Health Service, better and safer working conditions and shorter hours due to stronger trade unions. We were also able to retire at 60 or 65. The list goes on.

The birth control pill changed many things. During this transition period the youth knew nothing, compared to our modern world where the youth know everything about sex, well at least more than we knew, but the youngans seem to be lacking in common sense and a willingness to get their hands dirty. The young, and the parents of the young seem to think that it is their right to have a university education, and that the poor little bairns (children) should not be offended by anything.

This transition probably developed with the acceptance and the use of the contraceptive pill. During my adolescence and the onset of puberty, we were very much of the attitude that the boy takes the initiative and the young ladies say no, and the mark of our manhood was how, or if we could persuade the girls to say yes. There has always been a pressure within a peer group to show how manly we are, and how quickly we have made the transition into adulthood. During my youth and within my own environment, there were very few tests available to show our manliness; there were no wars to fight, we were not expected to go out into the bush and kill a lion. One of the few, and I have to say a popular way to show our manliness was how soon we lost our virginity, and how often we managed to persuade the ladies to say yes, and because of the importance of this we lied. I know exactly when I lost my virginity. I still have the receipt, and in the comments section it states "mercifully brief".

I think it is true to say that everyone lies about their sex life. The time, and with who we lost our virginity shouldn't be important, after all, it is at a time when we are young, stupid and impetuous, therefore many mistakes are made. I would say that nearly every first time we have sex it is a mistake, and almost definitely a disappointment for someone in some way. But our upbringing has an influence throughout our whole life, therefore, on the strength of all I have just said, how and why I lost my virginity isn't something to put on paper at this time, I have no need to embarrass or upset anyone, including me, now that I am in my 70s I'm sure nobody cares anyway, except perhaps the lovely Moi.

The more reliable and safe contraception available now has also meant that couples, and in particular the potential mother, can dictate when, how and if she is to become pregnant, and many chose not, or not as often, resulting in much smaller families, and the consequence of this is that any children produced become so precious that the parents are constantly trying to shield the poor little things from any harm, which I'm sure has the opposite effect in the long-run.

Enough chuntering for now, Let's get back to lovely ladies.

Early television programs that excited my loins were "A, For Andromeda" first shown in 1961, with Julie Christie. Also early natural history programs that ran in the 60s featured Hans and Lotte Hass who were makers of marine documentaries. Hans was particularly interested in sharks. The one program I remember was when they had caught a shark. They removed its heart, then placed the shark back in the water. We could see the fish slowly swimming away and the heart was shown still beating in the hand of one of the presenters. They were describing the shark's instinct for survival. This was at a time when respect for other living creatures wasn't as it is now, also little respect was shown for people watching the program, as I thought it was very gruesome and unnecessary. I liked Lotte though.

Armand and Michaela Denis also made wild life documentaries in the 50s and 60s. Their programs featured land animals of Africa, I was usually more interested in looking at Michaela, she was a bit of a stunner. Armand looked much older and I wondered what she was doing with an old fart like him. I was just being unkind and I am sure they thought the world of each other really. Armand was in fact an excellent photographer and wild life presenter but nothing like as good looking as Michaela. She was Deborah Kerr's double in the film King Solomon's Mines. Another of my very popular programs was "77 Sunset Strip". It was a very successful private detective team set on Sunset Strip, West Hollywood. One of the stars was Jacqueline Beer.

There is a theme running through all this, good looking ladies on screen. It developed into a fever pitch when "Barbarella" (released in 1968) was captured by Duran-Duran, and subjected her to his excessive machine or orgasmatron pipe-organ, with a view to slowly killing her to death with pleasure. But Barbarella was made of sterner stuff and she fused and melted the orgasmatron. She must have been a Yorkshire lass. Ursula Andress in the film "Dr. No" 1962, was also a big influence. A few years ago she auctioned the bikini she wore during that film and got more for it than she got for making the film. I dare not speculate as to what abuse that bikini is subjected to now.

My uncle Trevor was a manager of two cinemas in Huddersfield, The Picture House, and the Assoldo. If he saw me entering he would let me in for nothing. That's what happened the second time I saw Dr. No. A little while into the film he came to see me to ensure I was old enough. He said I had to be sixteen but as I was a big fifteen it'll be alright, but don't tell anyone. How times have changed. This film is now transmitted on television for anyone to watch, and in fact Moi and I watched it recently. It still holds up quite well as entertainment, but it's certainly very dated. I have avoided watching Barbarella again, as I know that will be rubbish and spoil my memory and imagination.

In the BBC's Omnibus series in 1970, they broadcast a Ken Russell film called "Dance of the Seven Veils". They wouldn't get away with it now. During the previous year Ken Russell directed a film called "Women in Love" staring Glenda Jackson" both very arty-farty films and which also got the self-appointed guardians of our moral fibre, in the form of Lord Longford and Mary Whitehouse in a right tizzy. We 'youngans' at the time assumed that there must be something wrong with these two.

There was a photo in the national press showing Lord Longford at a strip club with a buxom young lady wriggling her body in front of him. He was apparently touring Europe's red light districts so he could gather evidence for his "Anti Pornography Bill". He also openly advocated the release of Myra Hindley, one of the "Moors Murderers" and at the time the most hated woman in Britain. Myra Hindley was never released and died in 2002 aged 60. Even after spending 36 years in prison she was still so despised that no local undertakers would agree to handle her remains.

There is no evidence that I am aware of, that Mary Whitehouse attended a strip club. However, It is said that she thought Hughie Green, host of the very popular "Double Your Money", and "Opportunity Knocks" was the devil incarnate, and he among other BBC personalities were responsible for the moral collapse of the country, and she went on to suggest 'If only they could all be like that nice Mr. Savile'. Funny ole world init.

All these lovely ladies mentioned above, not including Mrs Whitehouse and Myra Hindley of course, but does include the afore mentioned (in an earlier edition of ramblings) Christa from Germany, ensured that I had a weakness that has endured for almost all of my life. However, there are signs that I am making a recovery at last. My biggest weakness has been reserved for the lovely Moi of course, I don't think I'll ever recover from that one.

Chapter 13: In search of the B17

Boing B17, Flying Fortress Duxford air museum late 1970s.

I have always been interested in military campaigns, wars and weaponry. When I was 15 years old, two of my school mates and I heard about a WW2 B17 Flying Fortress bomber that had crashed on Marsden Moor in 1945. Being innocent of the dangers, naive and romantic, we decided to climb up to Marsden Moor. I had never walked onto the moors before this time; however, it must be simple enough we thought – just head uphill from Marsden. So off we went one Saturday wearing only our normal playing-out clothing.

We were fully expecting the huge bomber to appear in front of us, perhaps one of the remaining engines still turning its last few revolutions, perhaps some weaponry scattered about waiting to be picked up and, even more exciting, a body or two to be discovered.

We were 15 years old and yet to learn to be careful of what to wish for; too stupid to see the fuller picture or the potential horror of the big bad world. We were simply looking for excitement.

We found our way onto the moor and were immediately amazed by the size and bleakness of the landscape. Marsden Moor,

Meltham Moor, and Black Hill are a tiny fraction of the northern end of the Peak District national park. Within an hour of leaving civilisation, or Marsden depending on the starting point, we can find ourselves in a landscape so foreboding, intimidating and threatening that we immediately realise how tiny and insignificant we are.

As far as the eye can see there are troughs, gullies and mountainous hills just waiting to swallow the foolish and unprepared, like an angry motionless sea of danger, frozen in time. Looking at it differently, there are views that fill the senses with wonderment: nothing but moorland as far as the eye can see, no civilisation to spoil nature, just gentle sounds, smells and fresh clean air that makes us feel we could live forever, or at least make us wish we could.

Undaunted by the landscape, us three young lads pressed on. If we carried on in a straight line, we must surely find the bomber, we thought.

As it often does in these parts, the mist began to fall and we were becoming hopelessly lost. Eventually after maybe a couple of hours, we came across some footprints in the peat. Logic and apprehension dictated that we should follow them, and so we did for another hour or so. Then to our amazement, these footprints doubled up. It took us a little while, but we eventually realised that we had been following our own footprints.

Apprehension turned to fear, as we could not see more than a hundred yards and had no idea which way to turn. As we stood in silence trying to work out in our own tiny minds what to do, we heard a vehicle in the distance. We then did the only sensible thing of the whole expedition up to that point and headed for the sound.

We found a road not far away but had no idea what road or which way to turn on it. We were getting tired, wet and miserable and decided to follow it downhill. After another hour, we came to the outskirts of Marsden.

As a measure of how lucky we had been, during the whole time from hearing that vehicle in the mist to entering Marsden, we did not see nor hear another vehicle on that road. This innocent adventure could so easily have ended as another tragic statistic.

The search for this crashed bomber has been on my minor bucket list ever since. In August 2021, the Lieutenant from our W.A.R.T.S. walking group discovered a walk arranged by the National Trust to four military crash sites on Black Hill, which is part of the moorland overlooking Huddersfield, including Marsden and Meltham Moors.

I had no idea there were four crash sites, but knowing this would include my bucket list B17 bomber, I jumped at the chance. The Lieutenant, the Colonel, and myself duly presented ourselves at the arranged Holme Moss car park, only to be told that the B17 is on Meltham Moor and would not be part of the walk. Gutted and crestfallen I nonetheless still joined in, and what an interesting walk it turned out to be.

One of the crash sites we visited that day involved the unfortunate demise of two pilots killed while flying their Gloster Meteor single seat fighter aircraft. They both crashed at the same time during an equipment training exercise in 1951. There were four Meteors in two pairs and the exercise was for two to practise 'detect and chase' on the other two. The exercise was called off because of bad weather and low cloud. Unfortunately, two radioed that they had seen a landmark and descended too far to investigate.

Like all the other crash sites we visited that day, they were so very near the summit. I would guess that this particular one was perhaps 50 feet from the top of the hill, but suddenly encountering 50 feet of undulating moorland peat, travelling at perhaps three or four hundred miles an hour, wouldn't have given these unfortunate pilots much of a chance. They probably never saw the ground, and death would have been instant. As for the bucket list of finding the B17, fate has dictated that this small ambition will perhaps never be satisfied.

Readers of my previous ramblings may be aware that I have had a very modest academic education. However, I recently heard that Sir Isaac Newton died a virgin, which means that I have one up on one of history's greatest scientific and knowledgeable minds ... because I'm not dead!

Chapter 14: Do men every really grow up?

It seems that the year of 1972 was, for me, further proof that they don't, and the following is an example of the lack of male maturity of me and my friends. It involves both Allen (Jinx) and the previously mentioned Dave Hill (Pill). Pill was visiting England, carrying out his customary showing off, and hired another MG sports car this time an MGB GT.

Pill had arranged that the old gang get together for a few beers, this time at the Junction Pub in Golcar. Beer was flowing and Pill suggested to Jinx, an amateur bike combination racer, that it would be a right good laugh if he took me for a spin in the MG.

Unbeknownst to me, the detailed instruction was to see if Jinx could frighten me. I never really discovered why. I'd shared a flat with Pill and had been on many spins around the block with him. As I was still 'immortal', he perhaps thought he would test my nerve.

The scene was set. I was in the left-hand passenger seat while Jinx was indeed trying his very best to scare me, squealing it around every bend. I was immaturely admiring his sliding technique, and after an appropriate period of time I asked if I could have a go. My own Austin A40 Farina was a very adequate small family car, but definitely not one to practice, or even attempt, sliding and squealing around bends. Happy just to get round the bend really.

We set off reasonably well. I was initially sensible enough to ask Jinx to instruct on the proper sliding technique. As we drove along Market Street, Milnsbridge, we then had to turn right up

Scar Lane and back to the pub. Jinx described this as "an ideal opportunity", promptly telling me, "second gear, floor it"; I thought I did as instructed but all the car seemed to do was silently drift sideways.

Back then, at the bottom of Scar Lane was a five story Victorian, stone, woollen mill. Only the pavement stood between the road and one of the very large stone windowsills, just right for sitting on while waiting at the adjacent but stop or before walking up the long, steep hill of Scar Lane, but not good for an MG set on a sideward trajectory. I mounted the curb and bounced onto the sill.

I had the sense to keep going before my mates in the local constabulary heard the clatter and came nosing around. There were police stations in every village at that time, with bobbies walking their regular beat. They were always turning up when least wanted in my world; strangely enough, I miss them now.

The only squealing now was the rear wheel arch pressed hard against the tyre. I lived just up the road at that time and called in to use my crow bar to lever the arch away from the wheel. Having done so we drove to and nonchalantly re-entered the pub.

Pill was fully expecting me to be shaking with fear, but Jinx was the most concerned, it was he who had narrowly avoided head-butting the stone windowsill. Jinx has recently said that he had experienced post traumatic stress for quite some time afterwards, my suggesting that he made an excellent air-bag for me didn't seem to make the memory any more enjoyable. I have to say in his defence, that like the rest of us, Jinx has also become a sensible member of society. He writes many letters of chuntering to our local rag and much of his chuntering concerns Margaret Thatcher, so that makes him a very sensible member of society in my book.

We told Pill that he may need a bit of filler before he returned it to the hire company, he didn't believe us of course, and the drinking continued. Pill kept asking, hoping we would soon give up trying to wind him up, but eventually he and some others went out to examine the damage. Every panel along the left hand side had damage, starting at the headlight and gradually becoming more severe towards the rear. The boot lid was buckled also.

I volunteered full responsibility, but as there had been an earlier conspiracy, both Pill and Jinx admitted most of the liability and I was let off the hook. Pill later said that he had paid an extra hire fee to cover damage. I was never sure if this was true, but luckily I had nothing to pay. I was very glad of that at the time as I had a young family and a mortgage, but as yet not fully grown up.

This visit by Dave Hill, and also his previous visit, resulted in two badly damaged MG sports cars. Other visits resulted in varying amounts of excitement, often involving the police trying to find him for some dodgy dealing. He disappeared at least twice from the Canadian authorities, and another time he ran away to the Cayman Islands but they caught up with him and he spent a couple of years in gaol. He also hid in Huddersfield for a period, having bought a hotel in the Midlands that mysteriously burnt down soon afterwards. The insurance didn't pay out for that one.

Pill was an intelligent and very interesting character, but he had a serious flaw in his makeup whereby he would rather earn a shifty, dishonest penny than an honest pound. It worked for him sometimes; he earned and lost at least two fortunes.

Pill standing in front of the wall papered with Korean won.
As of writing in 2023 the exchange rate was 0.00067 to the Pound.

Money would often colour Pill's judgment. This is him in 1968, standing in front of a wall he had papered with Korean Won. He had previously sent me 1,000 of the Korean won and suggested that I take the lads out for a meal.

Knowing that he could be very generous when he felt flush, I assumed that 1,000 Korean won was enough to buy several meals. I visited the bank in Huddersfield to change them into British cash, and the teller returned to tell me that they were worth approximately 2s/6d – about 25p.

I then saw an opportunity to get my revenge on Pill, never imagining that he would fall for it. I sent him a letter saying, "some meal for the lads, I only got £3/10s for the won". A telegram soon followed from Pill saying that he would be arriving in Huddersfield with a suitcase full of won, and I was asked to price up different bank exchange rates.

He hadn't fallen for it, had he? Surely he was just trying to prolong the joke wasn't he?

A few days later I softened and sent him a telegram saying that I was trying to outdo his sucker joke with a counter-sucker of my own. I later discovered from an independent source, much to my astonishment, that he had actually fallen for it. Greed and easy money had indeed clouded his judgment, and the above photo is part of the result.

He seems to have seen the funny side of it.

Chapter 15: The parachute jump

From left to right. Jenny my sister-in-law, The Colonel, Norky, Rachel and then Nick in colour co-ordinated sartorial elegance,

I think I'm correct in assuming that most people have a bucket list, something that they want to do, or achieve before they kick the bucket. From a very early age, one of mine was a parachute jump and in 1989 I had the opportunity.

My mate and previously mentioned Allen had been a skydiver for quite some time from the Grange-over-Sands airfield. He told me that they did training for first timers from his club. The word got around within my family and friends that this was happening, and some wanted in on the excitement. My daughter Rachel, little brother Nick and his wife Jennie, the colonel from the W.A.R.T.S and I were to be our team of jumpers. We were accompanied by family members clutching insurance policies.

The training was in two parts: theory, then practical. For the theory part, we were in a classroom and told all the things that can go wrong and what to do about it if it did. I was sure that much of this was designed to frighten us off, but apparently they had to go through all of this or they'd run the risk of losing their licence.

We were to be flying at 2,500 feet and using the static line system, whereby our ripcords were tethered to the Brittan Norman Islander aircraft, so all we *should* have to do is jump out and the parachute *should* open automatically.

We were told that immediately after we exit the aircraft we should shout, "one thousand, two thousand, three thousand check canopy". This is to ensure that the canopy has actually had time to open before we panic and pull the emergency shoot on our stomach. Even if we did panic, both shoots would *probably* still open, but as the canopies would be pushing against each other they'd not work to their best efficiency and we would land a second quicker than if only one parachute opened.

We were also shown photographs of what a canopy looks like from underneath, as well as photos of things that *can* go wrong. The instructor showed us a photo of some clouds, and just for a laugh, he said that this is what the canopy looks like if it doesn't come out of its bag. Oh how we laughed.

He also showed us a photo of a roman candle. This is when a line gets flicked over the centre of the canopy and it then collapses in on itself and instead of a parachute we have a spear. If this happened, we would hit the ground a second quicker than if it didn't open at all.

Some bright spark (not me), then asked, "How long do we have before we hit the ground?" The instructor said "thirteen seconds without a parachute". It slowly dawned on us all that we were to count three seconds before we looked at the canopy at all, and then if something did go wrong we'd have potentially only *nine* seconds to decide whether to deploy the reserve shoot, nine seconds! That's less time than sex, and about the same time as it takes to get into a car and fasten the seat belt. Oh how we stopped laughing then.

The practical training took place in the hanger. We were placed in teams of six, and each team practised jumping off platforms and were shown how to land. Then we were placed in our seating positions within a mock-up fuselage; there were no seats, just a hardboard floor for us to easily shuffle to our next jumping position.

As I was number one, I was sat next to the opening, the door having been removed. When it was time to jump, we had to shuffle with our legs out of the opening facing forward as best as we could, and when the instructor shouted "GO" we pushed out and took up the classic sky-diving position and began to shout the three second count.

All went well, nobody felt unable to carry on, and we were lucky that the weather conditions meant that we could do the jump immediately. Anything more than a five-knot wind and we would have had to go back another day, none of us relished that idea.

The previous photo is of us waiting our turn for the aircraft. We were told not to wander about and to fold our arms over our reserve parachute. This was to minimise the chance of equipment failure and accidental interference.

We took up our positions in the aircraft and off we went. The one thing I immediately noticed when I took up my jump position was how close the engine and landing gear was, neither of these being necessary in the mock-up. It looked like I would be jumping into one or the other; and jumping into a spinning propeller is *not* to be recommended.

Exiting the aircraft during my parachute jump 2,500 feet above Grange-Over-sands, 6th of August 1988.

Photograph courtesy of Allen Jenkinson.

This photo shows me exiting the aircraft immediately on the "GO" command, then starting my "one thousand" malarkey. I managed "two thousand" then "BLOODY HELL!" I don't remember if it was the excitement or the jolt of the canopy opening, but I definitely didn't manage the "three thousand, check canopy". All then went silent, except for an occasional flap of the parachute. The view was magnificent, over Morecombe Bay and the Irish Sea towards the Isle of Man, and inland over the Lake District.

The thing I didn't recognise was our landing target. During the photo training we were shown what to look for on the ground, so we could aim in that direction. The slit in the canopy is designed so that it can be turned into the wind. With no wind, these parachutes will travel at approximately five knots, which is an ideal landing speed for a novice. I couldn't recognise a thing on the ground, but thankfully the ground crew used loudspeakers to instruct us which way to turn, and we used toggles in the lines to do so. Even then, we all landed two or three hundred yards from the aiming mark.

We were all given scores during the debrief. My score was "ace", but the bravest by far was my little brother Nick. He doesn't like height or flying, so I can only assume he did it to support his big bruv.

Nick was the last person on our flight to jump. When it was his turn, he began to slowly – too slowly – shuffle towards the opening. At this point, the instructor intervened and gave him a "helping" hand, grabbing the nearest part of Nick's body and throwing him out of the aircraft.

We all landed safely and were buzzing with excitement as we gathered our equipment and made our way back to the hanger. All except Nick, who was just happy to be on the ground. Given how scared he was, he was far braver than I – so if I got an "ace" Nick deserved a "double ace"!

Our Brittan Norman Islander G-AXHE aircraft was written off following a crash just three years after our jump day. I believe no one was badly hurt.

Chapter 16: Arrival of Rachel

Moi and baby Rachel, summer 1969.

Before the baby boomer generation, potential parents knew little about proper, reliable or safe birth control. 'The Pill' was first developed in the US in the 50s, but didn't become widely used in Britain until the 60s. Even then, many women felt very uneasy about taking the pill.

My father was one of six siblings all reaching adulthood. My mother was also one of six, but only four reached adulthood. This was far from unusual. Out of my eight uncles and aunties, I had 22 cousins, but very few of them produced more than one child, and many none at all. This is almost exclusively (with some exceptions) the result of the birth control pill. Parents, and particularly the potential mothers, can determine whether or not to have a child, and many are choosing not to. And who can blame them? A life of pregnancy, discomfort, child rearing, worry and endless housework is understandably not for everyone.

Moi's first pregnancy ended with a miscarriage, but there were complications which meant that she may never have been able to become pregnant again. Following a two-year recovery period, we tried again. With Moi taking regular long rests, we were very fortunate to become proud parents of our lovely daughter Rachel.

With these difficulties, potential further heartbreak, and of course a serious risk to Moi's wellbeing, we decided one was enough. Moi went on the pill for ten years or so, and then I had the snip, described in probably too much detail in a previous ramble entitled "surgical adventures with the wedding tackle".

Having had 22 cousins meant that all the family gatherings, of which there were many, allowed us cousins to expand our friendship. Cousin Michael being just one. Unfortunately, Michael is one of five cousins who are no longer with us. All of them dying much too young, and all dying much younger than I am now.

Cousin Michael was a lovely fella. He was the eldest son of Dad's eldest brother, making him quite a few years older than me. He became the older brother that I never had.

Michael was a big lad, probably well over 20 stone with the same pear body shape as his mother, although he wasn't a great deal taller. Michael liked uniforms; he had a wardrobe full of 'em. As a boy he had cub and scout uniforms; then in his youth became a sea cadet, later to become an officer/instructor. He was also a special police constable and an ambulance driver; and until his retirement, he was a paramedic. I suspect that there was a small mill somewhere dedicated to manufacturing Michael's uniforms.

We all probably suffer occasionally from the inability to see in advance what space our bodies will fit through and Michael was no exception. He and his fellow paramedic colleague Ian once attended a motor vehicle accident where the car was upside down, with the injured driver still inside. Michael began to crawl through the broken rear window and was just about to get his lower half stuck, when Ian dragged him back out saying "silly bugger, you'll never get that arse through there". Ian managed to get the driver out and all survived with their own memories.

Michael often told me that when sat with a patient laid out in the back of his ambulance following a motor vehicle accident, at some stage the patient will inevitably say, "I had right of way ya know".

Rachel was born at 03.50 on the 15th. of June 1969. During the previous day Moi was increasingly experiencing labour pains, and by the evening, contractions had reached one per minute – the time we were told to initiate the birth procedure. As we couldn't get a signal on the mobile phone in 1969, I had to run about a quarter of a mile to the nearest phone box to summon the ambulance to take Moi to St. Luke's Maternity Hospital.

Then, an extremely unexpected surprise: when the ambulance turned up, who should be driving it but Cousin Michael! Bundling Moi in the back, we arrived at the hospital without bother and we were ushered into the ward. Michael left me to see Moi to her bed and the nurse sent me away, saying, "Okay Mr Norcliffe, off you go now, ring in the morning to see what you've got".

I was more than happy to leave. It was a time when father's were not expected to stay and watch. In my humble opinion (formed mostly from some of my previous experiences with hospitals), if you can walk out of a hospital under your own steam, you should do so at the first opportunity.

Another aspect that hadn't crossed my mind was something that my mate told me, perhaps a little lacking in romance. He had been persuaded or felt obliged to be present at the birth of his youngest child and he said, "It was like watching my favourite pub burn down'

Good old Cousin Michael was waiting to take me back home. I seem to remember that another reason I was glad to get home was that there was an anticipated kickerball game on television. I have looked back to see what match this could have been on Saturday the 14th of June 1969, and I can't find it now; perhaps I was delirious with excitement or alcohol.

I rang on the morning of the 15th and was told that I had a daughter, that mother and child were doing well, and that I could visit that afternoon. I duly arrived and was ushered along a glass-sided corridor, on the other side of which was a long row of newly born bundles of joy in white canvas cots. A nurse held up one child. It actually could have been any child, but was apparently my daughter. It was all very detached. Even though I remember it well, the cold, formal and impersonal nature of the experience put a bit of a dampener on the occasion. I don't know what they could have done to make it more positively eventful. I was of course overjoyed with our new daughter. I think I would have been equally overjoyed with a son. However, my recent relationship with dad was not perfect, and I had certain concerns that my relationship with my son would turn out the same.

I have to say that any relationship I would have had with a son, could not have been better than both me and Moi have with Rachel.

At that time of Rachel's birth, mothers stayed in bed for approximately ten days, or until the uterus returned to its normal position. I remember being kicked in my uterus during a karate competition, I dropped like a stone, I felt like lying down for ten days as well.

On Moi's return to the happy family home, she told me about the birth. When the staff thought it was time to get Moi into the delivery room, she was asked to walk up to the first floor and while climbing the stairs, her waters broke – that promoted her to walk a bit quicker!

The older I get, the more I find my waters breaking at times, perhaps my 'uterus' never did go back to its normal position.

Chapter 17: At last ticking off the B17 from the bucket list

As described in a previous Ramblings episode, the 1962 expedition to find the B17 bomber on Marsden Moor with my two schoolmates had been unsuccessful, and since it had so very nearly resulted in our demise, the dread of it happening again had put me off any further attempt. But the strange thing about the human mind is that we often come to believe that the things that once frightened us must be faced again. A 'straight back in the saddle after a fall' type of attitude. This is how discovering the B17 bomber on Marsden Moor had developed in my tiny mind, and for some 60 years that's where it stayed. When the chance came to lay this fear to rest which had also proved unsuccessful. I became a little convinced that the gods were against me. Because of this, I became even more determined.

I had suggested to the W.A.R.T.S. walking group that we try to find this bomber, not only to fulfil my bucket list, but because it could also be an interesting journey into another part of the moor. Arrangements were made, but by the day of the trip, various pathetically lame excuses meant that only Lieutenant Forager and myself were willing to trek across the moor and risk the wrath of the gods.

The weather conditions would have been very similar to the day of the crash, and similar to that day in 1962. Low cloud and mist, slight drizzle and more than a little miserable.

B17 crash site found at last. 14th of September 2021.

The B17, nicknamed 'The Flying Fortress' was built by the Boeing company for the US Army Air Corps in the mid 1930s. Nearly 13,000 were produced. It was a large, four-engine, heavy bomber, similar in size and performance to our own Lancaster bomber. However, the B17 sacrificed its bomb load for defensive capabilities: it had guns at the top, bottom, front, back and both sides, hence the nickname Flying Fortress. Each US bomber crew gave their aircraft a name, usually chosen by the pilot, and often named after the pilot's mother. The wreckage we visited that day was called *Barbara Jane*.

Barbara Jane was on a test flight in April 1945, having had two new engines fitted. The crash happened when the crew got lost in the Pennine mist and descended to find a landmark. Because it was a test flight, there were only five crewmembers on board that day. All five survived, though unfortunately two suffered serious injuries, and one died a few years later from complications resulting from his injuries.

The Forager and I parked next to a footpath that we knew took us to West Nab. This was the starting point suggested by the National Trust guide during the crash site walk on Black Hill the previous month. He said it was easy – just follow a straight line from that trig point on West Nab to Deer Hill.

Unfortunately, we could see neither West Nab nor Deer Hill, but the footpath thankfully took us to the trig point without problems. Then with the help of a combination of my traditional compass, but mainly The Forager's phone app, we managed to walk in a straight line north, north-west over the moor.

There were no landmarks, just undulating heather and stream-cut gullies as far as the eye could see, which was no more than 100 yards. It was little more than a mile over the moor, but turned out to be a good workout. From the summit of West Nab, we didn't have any paths taking us in the correct direction.

I suspect that there were no paths because the area of the crash site is in the danger area of Deer Hill shooting range. So we kept our heads down, even though it would have been hard for anyone to make out a target to aim at that day, apart from perhaps being close enough to throw a rock at us.

The Forager's app kept telling us that we were getting closer. We peered into the misty gloom, hoping for the best but fearing that we could easily miss it by only yards and then get shot by a wayward bullet or rock from Deer Hill.

We kept checking our compass and app every 20–30 paces. Every time we had to negotiate a stream-cut gulley, which took us off course and we again checked our direction.

I pride myself in being able to find my way home, in normal conditions, but also knew that these conditions were far from normal. After negotiating a particularly deep and tricky gully, I tested my natural direction-finding skill and without referring to the compass or app I pointed to where I thought north was. To my dismay, I discovered that I was pointing south, and this was just a few minutes after previously checking.

We quickly corrected our bearings and continued further and further into the moor. The Forager again checked his app and said we are very close to the co-ordinates on the website. I walked a few yards further and looked over a slight crest and, as if by magic, there it was. We had scored a bull's-eye, every bit as accurately as the sharpshooters at Deer Hill.

To get back, all we needed to do then was walk due south and we would hit the road we had left two hours earlier. We did better than that: we found the trig point on West Nab and from there followed the footpath down to the car. Justifiably elated and very satisfied, albeit moist! To celebrate my fulfilled bucket list, the Forager treated me to bacon butty and an ice cream sundae, a strange combination, one may think, but it was a strange day.

The compass alone would have kept us in a straight line there and back, but without the app and the correct co-ordinates, we would have had little to no chance of finding the crash site. I had always thought this site was on Marsden Moor, but in fact it's on Meltham Moor, although nobody would be able to tell the difference.

A happy and fulfilling day.

Chapter 18: Three day week, banter, nicknames and pranks

I will avoid trying to justify the rights and wrongs of the industrial disputes of the 1970s, of which there were many. I'll happily leave that to others who are much more qualified to do so. What I do feel qualified to write about is how they affected me.

I've previously written about the firefighters' strike of 1977 in a previous ramble, firefighting, floating gerbils and running about a bit in book one. There was also the electricians' work-to-rule in December 1970, where we had regular blackouts. Whole areas were just switched off, and homes, hospitals and offices were run by candlelight or emergency generators.

I'm sure people under 40 years old would struggle to imagine what life would be like without smart phones, iPads, televisions, radios, computers, battery chargers, lighting in the home or street. Heavy industry and shops that required electricity had to hang around until the power came back on again. Luckily this dispute only lasted a few days.

However, another dispute – this time involving the miners and railway workers, and their work-to-rule in December 1974 – resulted in the 'three day week'. All commercial business, with few exceptions such as hospitals and newspaper printing presses, could only work on three consecutive days per week. The measures were introduced by the then Conservative government as a means of conserving electricity supplies, which were restricted because of the industrial action.

At the time of the three-day week I was working at Brook Motors, Huddersfield. Owing to jobs in the textile trade becoming more and more scarce, I made the move to another aspect of engineering and became a welder/fitter at the company. After mergers and take-overs, its full and proper name was Hawker Sidley Brook Crompton Parkinson Motors, but if someone asked where I worked, they would have walked off before I got that lot out. So we just called it by its previous name: Brook Motors.

After each of our projects was finished, we collected new drawings from the drawing office. Many were adapted from earlier drawings, therefore included both imperial and metric measurements. Not that each measurement was shown in both imperial and metric, but the older section was imperial and the newer, adapted sections were in metric. What could possibly go wrong? We had to keep our wits about us, or we could easily have a roller conveyor emerging from the gent's toilet or a crane leg secured in front of an emergency exit.

The merger of number six (the mechanical maintenance fitters) and number ten (the welder/fitters), brought together many who were young and fresh out of apprenticeships. As a consequence, practical jokes and banter were commonplace. Much of this would not be tolerated in the modern workplace. I can't remember any instances of racism, sexism or homophobia, certainly no more than we were used to outside of our work environment, and much of this is also quite rightly regarded as wrong now. I seem to remember all other forms of banter were fair game at work at that time.

Practical jokes were many and varied. They could also be described as bullying, but we were all subjected to these jokes in equal measure. The welding benches were big solid steel constructions with the arc welding earth permanently connected. If anybody came along to bother us and leaned on the bench, we could grab the electrode end of the welder in one hand and accidentally touch them with our other hand and give them a very amusing jolt.

Jeff (Bigs, because he was tall) was our store man. He rode to work on a pushbike with a wooded box on the back for the occasional spare part he'd spirit away. Periodically, when Jeff had been given time to forget the previous episode, someone would remove what was in the box and fill it with scrap metal instead. We always enjoyed that prank! Poor old Bigs must have been knackered by the time he'd peddled ten pounds of scrap home.

We also played a game whereby we'd ask someone to place their head inside a cardboard box about the size of a television, having already cut a hole in the front the size of a television screen. The object was to appear as if we were on television looking out at the audience and whistle. Yes, all we had to do was whistle. Many lads tried it but nobody, not a single person, managed to whistle.

Using nicknames was one of the milder forms of banter, based on what we were like or something notable that we had done. Hymas' real name was Michael; other notables were Fruitbat, Father Jim, Jim Lad and Beaker. Mine was Petal.

It is over 40 years ago now and I can only remember some origins of the nicknames. Fruitbat was quite mad of course; Father Jim was called Jim and was the foreman; Jim Lad was also called Jim but was not a foreman. Unfortunately, Beaker looked just like his namesake from the Muppet Show, from the mid to late 70s. I was called Petal because I called everybody 'petal' or 'love' at that time, and it fitted nicely with Peter (Peter Petal). There was one lad called Sillick, I have no idea where that nickname came from but I do remember that his last name was Hunt.

We were all subjected to this banter, which was to some extent abuse of course. But I'm sure it helped us tolerate the difficult working conditions of heavy industry, and it certainly helped when coping with the 12-hour day.

At the start of the 1970s, I had a three-year-old marriage, a two-year-old mortgage and a six-month-old child. "Pressure, what pressure?"

Incidentally, our first mortgage in early 1968 was £6/1s/8d, per month, (about £6.08 in today's money). That was every month mind. It may not seem much now, but I was still an apprentice in the textile industry at the time, on about £12/14 per week. Also because I was under 21, my dad had to sign as guarantor so we could get the mortgage.

Two years later when my wife Moi was also 20, she entered our village library attempting to get a library ticket. We'd been married for three years by that point and Moi had our one-year-old daughter Rachel in a pushchair with her when she went in.

The jobsworth behind the counter would not give her a library card without a responsible adult acting as guarantor. So Moi had to trail to the other end of the village to her dad's, then go grovelling back to jobsworth with the signed form.

The three day week, January to March 1974, regulations meant that companies were allowed to work no more than 12 hours per day for those three consecutive days. I therefore worked for 36 hours per week, 12 of which were counted as time and a quarter overtime, as our normal working day was eight hours. Then we were allowed to sign on (dole) for the rest of the week, which at that time included Saturday morning. The result was that I was actually a few pounds better off each week, despite working fewer hours than our normal 40. However, even though we were getting normal break times, working in a manual job for 12 hours in one stretch was quite tiring. Still, by the time the dispute was settled (just over two months later), we were getting quite used to it. So getting back to a five-day week had its own difficulties. Working 12-hours a day was a long day; working five days a week felt like a long week.

We had no choice of course, and as I remember we weren't consulted on the matter. On balance, I preferred the three day week, particularly if I would be paid more.

Chapter 19: Beers and pubs

On very special occasions, and sometimes perhaps on a Sunday, my dad would have a bottle of ale with his dinner. The first time I remember this happening was one Christmas at Bolster Moor, so I would be no older than seven. The reason I remember it was because Dad put a small amount in a glass for me, perhaps no more than an inch, but it was very special. The taste was something very different, and very occasionally a guest beer will evoke that same, very happy memory from all those years ago. My memory of the beer my dad liked on those occasions came in a dark green/brown long necked bottle with a Bakelite screw cap.

Beer has been a standard beverage for hundreds of years. In fact, for many decades it was much safer to drink than water. The fermentation process during the making of beer killed many harmful bacteria that were common in village drinking water. Traditionally the men would drink the beer produced in the first mash (a porridge-like mixture of grain and water where the sugars eventually turn into alcohol). The mash would then be used again to produce a weaker beverage, and then used a third time to produce a drink weak enough to give to children. Physical work out in the fields would require the men to drink a gallon of their strong ale every day.

During or soon after the Victorian era, efficient sanitation and clean drinking water became the norm, and beer drinking then became a leisure activity. Many householders were brewing beer and giving up areas of their houses as meeting places for locals to gather, socialise and drink beer. This developed into what we now recognise as a pub (public house). History often goes round in circles, and many of our pubs have now closed and been converted into housing.

Over the last 100 years or so, beers have evolved several times. Fashions also change. My dad's generation often drank from half pint glasses and the mild beers that use fewer hops during brewing were very popular. Gradually the bitter beer became the only option from many pubs, and mild beer has now become a minority sport. A popular beer option during my formative years was a pint of 'mixed' half bitter and half mild.

Then came the dreaded keg beer. This beer is pasteurised (heat treated) to stop further fermentation, and carbon dioxide is added to give it fizz. It was first developed for export to India but then, through the work of the devil, it became popular in Britain. I suspect that this went a long way towards the demise of the mild beers.

Luckily, through the gallant work of, among others, the Society for the Preservation of Beers from the Wood (SPBW) established in 1963, and since 1971 the Campaign for Real Ale(CAMRA), we now have many real, proper ales to choose from. Microbreweries are popping up in old run-down mills all over the Colne Valley and surrounding areas.

Unfortunately, the beers available in the pubs my biking mates and I were welcome in during the 1960s tended to be the ones selling keg beers. The most memorable (notorious) beers were Watney's Red Barrel, Worthington 'E', Whitbread Tankard, Brew Ten, Ind Coope Double Diamond, Younger's Tartan and Courage Tavern. There have been several studies into why keg beer became popular. It was, after all, weaker, more expensive and less flavoursome than the traditional hand pump beers. The most popular conclusion to such studies was that "it had more fizz".

Bottled beer has been around for hundreds of years, and canned beers since the mid-1930s. Ind Coope Long Life is said to have been among the first. I remember the first appearance of Watney's Party Seven, a can containing seven pints, strangely enough, first produced in 1968. It was a novel idea and thought ideal for parties, but it was horrible. Before then, us regular partygoers might club together and buy a five or ten-gallon traditional wooden barrel of beer. The technique was to let it settle for a day before attempting to hammer the big brass tap into the barrel without it flying across the room and wasting much of the beer.

The popular beers that were produced locally were Bentley and Shaw of Huddersfield, Samuel Webster's of Ellend, Timothy Taylor's of Keighley, Joshua Tetley's of Leeds, Wilson's of Manchester and Sam Smith's of Tadcaster. Notable exceptions to local breweries were Bass, later to become Bass Charrington, Worthington's, Stones, and Guinness.

All these beers were of varying quality and were often tolerated rather than liked because the pubs selling these beers were within easy walking distance or run by a landlord/landlady who provided a very friendly and pleasant atmosphere. Some beers even had the reputation of being able to give you varying degrees and quality of hangovers and some could give you a right good clear-out.

One of the pubs we frequented was The Commercial in Hoyle House, if we felt like slumming it a bit, and didn't care too much about spoiling their reputation. But if we felt a little posh, or wanted to impress the ladies, we frequented The White House in Slawit, Blue Ball at Norland and Castle Hill in Newsome. All of these are now closed. There may be a common denominator here somewhere. Not only was The Commercial closed, but it was quickly demolished, and the space left doesn't seem big enough to fit a garage never mind a pub. Perhaps like Dr Who's Tardis, it was bigger inside than out.

The Commercial in Hoyle House was a regular venue for our rowdier gatherings, with much alcohol consumed. Keg beers were sold (Brew Ten, if memory serves) and because it was horrible, we felt obliged to drink enough for it to become tolerable, which started to happen after about three pints. Then each pint after the third was counted as double and so on. While very unpleasant, this beer did still contain alcohol and as a result this particular pub seems to be where the silliest and most juvenile incidents took place, most of which I don't feel brave enough to mention in Norky's Ramblings, not even in the 'Do men ever grow up?' mini-series.

All I will say is that all fines, sentences, punishment and penalties were carried out in a timely and manly manner without complaint. When we were caught, that is – when they were caught, I mean, of course. I'm sure I don't have to point out again that I myself was completely innocent of even any minor incident in which I may have been involved. I just happened to be stood close by while others were acting in a drunken rowdy manner.

I am proud to say that I am still friends with many of the survivors, who with the help of Norky's maturity and guidance, have grown up to be fine fellows. I think the ladies may have had some part to play also.

Chapter 20: The Devil's music

As my big sis Rhondda is five years older than me, and strangely enough, always has been, I was greatly influenced by her choice of music, and during her teenage years 1955 to 1962 there was an explosion of pop (popular) music aimed at, and performed by, the young. As the country was recovering from WW2, and the influence of recent rationing was still very much biting into everyday life, much of this choice of music was a protest deliberately aimed at the establishment. This kind of statement of opposition and protest through music has gone on for generations.

An example today would be rap music, which I cannot understand nor appreciate. But, of course, it isn't aimed at me – in fact, it's deliberately written to break free from old fuddy-duddies like me. I'm sure rap artists would be mildly upset if I did like it. Fortunately, nowadays young musicians don't depend on us oldies for their income. It was different in Mozart's day. When Emperor Joseph II criticised the young composer for being too intense and using too many notes, tremors will have been felt in the financially fragile Mozart household.

Jazz from the US became very popular and from this skiffle developed. Lonnie Donegan's "Rock Island Line" 1956, was a great hit. It is said the he was the first performer to introduce the guitar as the main focal instrument into Britain.

In 1958, John Weatherby, Rhondda's boyfriend, now husband, joined the Comets, a skiffle group. The following photo was taken the year after and was pretty much the standard of the day: all acoustic guitars, no drums, John on the left playing bass/rhythm on an acoustic six-string guitar, and a tea chest bass, comprised of a tea chest, a brush handle, and a length of string. Some skiffle group rhythm sections used a washboard, which is a wooden frame with a corrugated tin middle section, originally designed to wash clothing. The player placed thimbles on their fingers and rattled them up and down the washboard. This instrument sounded just like you would expect – a right racket.

The Comets 1959. Photo provided by John Weatherby.

The only music shop in Huddersfield at that time was Woods and, as described previously, Woods did not look favourably upon the noisy hip-shaking groups of the time, seeing them as being in league with the Devil.

The following photo is of John in his garden posing in his best cool, rock and roll stance.

John posing outside his home in Flat House, Linthwaite. c1958.
Photo provided by John Weatherby.

Guitars were not easy to come by. This is John's first and it cost 10 guineas (£10.50) from a furniture shop in Huddersfield. This guitar was also my first after John very kindly gave it to me when I was 12 years old.

Initially the budding rock stars of the 50s and 60s played in youth clubs or village halls, but eventually bigger venues meant amplification was required. They could acquire and afford to buy pickups to fit on the body of their acoustic guitars, but had to build their own amplifiers, often from valves and speakers destined for the television and radio industry, and of course requiring lots of know-how. 'Necessity is the mother of invention' and all that.

John appears to be playing the chord of C. If a player could manage the chord sequence C, A minor, F and G, then there were dozens of ballads available at their fingertips (literally). But it was only if they felt really ambitious and learned the chord sequence A, E and B7 that they could consider themselves a guitarist. B7 is an awkward bugger, but if mastered, it opened up a whole new world of rock and roll. I also find anything in the key of B to be awkward, too many sharps and flats. Something should be done! probably starting with my musical ability and education.

The term 'rock and roll' originally came from the US jazz world and was used as a metaphor in the 1920s for dancing but also for sex, which of course is another example of pop music rattling the establishment cage.

Radio Luxembourg was where the youth were getting their pop music entertainment, the BBC being very reluctant to embrace the work of the Devil for some time yet. The brighter musicians within the groups would learn the tune, lyrics and chords by listening to them over the airwaves and arranging them for their own groups.

John eventually joined the Phantoms, a group that quickly became well established and popular all over the north of England. Their excellent lead guitarist, Dave Hesp, often said that John was accepted into the group because his brother Stuart had a Morris J2 van, big enough for the whole group and their equipment. This is hotly disputed by both Rhondda and John, and I suspect it was just a bit of banter, but a good story anyway. Stuart Weatherby was quickly promoted from van driver to manager until the group needed a more professional agent and management setup.

Dave Hesp was a joiner and made a number of his own solid six-string guitars. He also made John's first proper solid bass guitar. In 1961, Dave bought a Fender Stratocaster. There were very few in the country at that time and even though the Phantoms had toured and played with many bands, it was the first time they had seen a 'Strat' other than on a cover of a Buddy Holly LP.

Not only were solid bodied guitars easier to make, they also reduced the feedback that was found to be a problem when playing acoustic guitars through an amplifier. Feedback happens when a sound from a speaker is again picked up by the acoustic body of the guitar and then amplified again, very quickly resulting in a high-pitched squeal.

The Phantoms 1961. Photo provided by John Weatherby.

This photo is of the Phantoms taken in late 1961 sporting their new Blonde Vox AC30 amplifiers. Not getting much support in their hometown music shop, the group had bought instruments from Barrett's of Manchester for some time. Even then, it required Mr Barrett himself to drive to London to pick up these Vox AC30s. The Phantoms were the first group to use these amps after the Shadows in 1961.

John left when they turned professional and the Phantoms then toured military airbases in Europe.

At around that time they produced a record at the Joe Meek studio in London. As there was a copyright problem, the Phantoms had to change their name, and it was Joe Meek who suggested 'The Dynamics', which was the name they appeared under in August 1964 on *Thank Your Lucky Stars*. Produced by *ABC Television* from 1961 to 1966, it was essential viewing for millions of British teenagers. Jimmy Savile introduced them as 'The Dynamos'. Sadly, it was discovered all too late that Jimmy Savile's inability to read an autocue was the least of his problems.

I often acted as a roadie on many of the Phantoms' gigs around the north of England, the most notable being on Wednesday 13 February 1963. Not only did Rhondda give birth to John's first child during that evening, but Steven was also my first nephew. And, if that wasn't enough, the Phantoms played at Barnsley Baths alongside the Spotnicks, a Swedish group who specialised in instrumentals, not too dissimilar to the Shadows.

The Phantoms had been playing many of the Spotnicks' numbers at that time, including *Orange Blossom Special*, but the Spotnicks' manager refused permission for the Phantoms to play this particular number that evening. As they were not going to play it themselves – he gave a lame excuse that the building had too much exposed metalwork which would interfere with their equipment. The general consensus was that this was rubbish and so the Phantoms played it anyway in their last set.

John described the Spotnicks as initially being very standoffish and superior, but strangely enough after the Phantoms played *'Orange Blossom Special'*, their attitude changed immediately to a very friendly respect.

Chapter 21: A Luddite and proud

I am often accused of being a Luddite, there are several quite legitimate reasons for this. I will list just a few. I refuse to waste my brass on a Smart Phone, they manipulate people's lives way too much for my liking, they dominate and/or interrupt conversation, they answer disputes and troublesome questions within seconds and immediately eliminate the search that often took days to answer and therefore remove the cockiness associated with spending all that time proving someone wrong. I remember often spending all evening with my mates arguing about just one subject without a satisfactory conclusion, and if a smart phone was available I would have been proven correct immediately, surely there's little satisfaction in that.

I do not hold with this social media malarkey either, the whole thing is in league with the Devil. They are influencing conspiracy theories, false truths and downright lies, and have a detrimental effect on youngans' body image. Social media is not for grumpy Norky thank you very much.

In my humble opinion, I am much too old to pretend to be modern, there are also many things in this modern world that dictate that I am just the right generation to be grumpy about it. The "Baby Boomers" have earned the right to criticise these youngans of today and we are very happy to do so, and be grumpy about it.

By-eck!! I feel better for that.

Now that I've had a little purge, I will write something about the proper Luddites, who were very much associated with the Colne Valley.

The Luddite movement started around 1811, and emerged within an atmosphere of constant difficulties , where starvation and being unable to house their families was a constant threat. Life was harsh and if that wasn't enough, so was justice. There was no welfare state, therefore if the bread winner within the family could not get work then the family starved. Britain was still basically a rural economy, but industrialisation and capitalism were beginning to take hold, which caused a certain amount of destabilisation.

Things began to come to a head when Enoch Taylor, a blacksmith from Marsden developed a textile cropping machine that did the work of ten men, groups of excitable young men saw these machines as the last straw and began a campaign of destruction. One of the great ironies of the time was that the large sledge hammer that they used to break up these machines was also produced by the blacksmith Enoch Taylor. The mantra at the time was "Enoch make em, and Enoch brake em".

The late 1700s and early 1800s was a period of particular turmoil, harsh living and working conditions for the masses ran alongside the justice system that treated the same people with the most heart-breaking sentencing for what we would regard now as a very minor offence. The threat of deportation to Van Diemen's Land (Tasmania) for stealing a loaf of bread was not unheard-of. But there was always a chance of returning when their sentence was carried out. Many of The Luddites did not get that chance.

The origin of the name "Luddit" has drifted into folk-law. One explanation seems to stem from the frame braking perpetrators blaming Ned Ludd, possibly Edward Ludlam as the ringleader, as a person by this name had already a reputation of breaking stocking frames during a fit of rage. On the other hand, it is also said that this Ned Ludd incident took place many years before the Luddite movement was conceived. Also to confuse history further, there is little to no evidence that Ned Ludd, or Edward Ludlam ever existed.

To combat the growing threat of the Luddites, mill owners were employing local militia, even using cannons to protect their mills and livelihoods. One incident at Rawfold's Mill in Dewsbury where the owner, William Cartwright, had anticipated an attack and had heavily defended his mill, resulted in two Luddites being killed and many more injured. The official verdict for these deaths were Justifiable homicide" which resulted in mass demonstrations. This incident is described in the book "Shirley" written by Charlotte Bronte 1816-1855. Probably described to her by her father Patrick who was curate within the parish of Dewsbury from 1809 to 1815.

During the run-up to this period, the French revolution had been raging from 1789 to 1799. Then the Napoleonic wars 1803 to 1815, were demanding men and money. The Mad King George was the present Monarch and our Prime Minister Spencer Percival was assassinated in May 1812. All this meant that many MPs were concerned that this was going to develop into anarchy and as many governments did, and still do, our government responded with violence of their own, and rushed the "Frame Braking Bill" through parliament in 1812, whereby anyone found guilty of braking textile machinery could be sentence to death.

Lord Byron in his maiden speech to the House of Lords, spoke out against this Bill, saying that "the value of a life is worth less than a stocking frame".

With this background, in April 1812, four idealistic young croppers, George Mellor, William Thorpe, Thomas Smith and Benjamin Walker lay waited in hiding at Lane End, then ambushed and mortally wounded William Horsfall, a mill owner from Marsden, as he left the Warren House pub and continued home six miles along the packhorse route following his weekly visit to the Huddersfield market.

William Horsfall seems to have had a strange disregard for his personal safety. He was a mill owner that used much of the equipment hated by the Luddites, he built a substantial wall protecting his Marsden property that included shooting slots, he was a known and vociferous hater of the Luddite movement, yet rode on horseback through the centre of the Luddite heartland almost as if he was provoking something.

In January of the following year, these four were captured, convicted and three were hung, Benjamin Walker turned kings evidence and survived. Fourteen others were also hanged, none of which had anything to do with the William Horsfall murder, there was also little to no evidence suggesting that they had broken any frames either, but they were known ne're-do-wells and were convicted of being Luddite supporters. The authorities had to make an example, and in so doing knew that they would not do it again, whatever it may be.

The hanging of these 17 men left approximately 70 children fatherless. Seven siblings were made orphans as their mother had died a few months previously.

There were some spasmodic outbreaks for another couple of years, but essentially the Luddite movement was over, they could not stop progress. There were no improvements in living standards for the poor, and in many cases they became even worse off.

Some one hundred years after his murder, a street was named after William Horsfall. However, The packhorse route, Lane End and the Warren House pub have long gone, replaced by Blackmoorfoot Road, Tom Lane, housing and shops. The Luddite headquarters was in Longroyde Bridge, near the start of the packhorse route on which William Horsfall passed every week. Another Warren House pub built nearby on Manchester Road, is also now closed. All these names and places are at the eastern end of the Colne Valley and are approximately two miles from my home. Enoch Taylor's blacksmith shop and William Horsfall's mill was a further six miles to the western end of the Colne Valley in Marsden.

There is a reconstructed set of stocks near Marsden church, no doubt used during the Luddite period for people who were late paying their rent, or looked at the local gentry in a funny way. Oh how I would like to see their return, for people who constantly play rowdy music, who don't treat or train their pet dogs properly or who completely block the pavement with their cars.

Another purge, I feel even better now.

Chapter 22: Bike tours, part one with friends

In 1987, we decided to buy a property with a bigger garden further up the road in Golcar. The plan was to build a garage in the garden for my building materials. I had been self employed since 1981 and had been using a succession of old Transit vans as mobile sheds, which was proving increasingly inconvenient.

Rachel was 18 years old at that time and lived in the same property her whole life, as a consequence, she did not look forward to the move. Rachel has always been very independent and saw this as an opportunity to branch out on her own, and did.

Moi hated the idea of Rachel leaving home, very much like mothers have over many generations. I, on the other hand, encouraged her to crack on. I had done the same at the similar age, so had my sister Rhondda and our brother Nick. Although in Rhondda's case it was to get married. But I still maintain that around eighteen is a very civilised age to leave home.

When Rachel was born in 1969, it soon became obvious that owning a motorcycle for pleasure was selfish and wasteful, and it had to go in favour of a small family car.

When Rachel left home Moi and I thought it an opportunity to regain our youth and see what excitement another bike will bring. I looked around for something sensible and avoided the, and all too often fatal trap that many born-again bikers fall into, and jump on a two wheeled rocket ship.

Our born-again bike was a Kawasaki GT 550. Perfectly adequate bike to travel around Britain, but as we were loving it so much, we branched out and bought a Kawasaki GT 750. This was the bike on which we took our first foreign trip. Luckily our good friends Philip and Roberta had been touring abroad many times and took us under their wing, and we were very glad they did, as it opened up a whole new chapter in our lives. This first tour started with an overnight ferry trip from Plymouth to Santander. In itself this was an adventure. We toured along the coast of Northern Spain touching Portugal then returned through the relatively mountainous area of Spain and up the length of France, 2,500 miles in total. This certainly broke the ice as regards motorcycle tours.

An Englishman abroad.

On our return we killed some time waiting for our ferry on a beach at Saint-Malo. We soon discovered to our alarm that it was a topless beach, it may even have been a nude beach but I wasn't allowed to look too closely. This photo is of me pretending to be an Englishman abroad and being offended by all this naked flesh.

We soon discovered that we needed more luggage space, to be more accurate, it was Moi's discovery. We then progressed to a Kawasaki GTR 1000. A very good touring bike with plenty of luggage space.

Unfortunately, this bike also suffered from a shrinking luggage capacity. We then progressed to the biggest bike available at the time, a Honda Goldwing 1500.

Moi had both panniers and the huge top-box, I had a small plastic bag fastened to the top-box and both side pockets on my jacket for all my stuff.

This action photo was taken on one of the very few easy sections of road through the southern French Alps, 2012.

I joined the International Motorcycle Tour Club to further my knowledge and support during any future foreign tours. The main reason I joined was because their northern England monthly meetings were held in Huddersfield. We became very friendly with the I.M.T.C. members and in particular Geoff and Jacquie. Geoff was a compulsive organiser of foreign bike tours, and bloody good he was at it. We must have done ten of Geoff's tours, which included many of their friends, which in turn became our friends.

The regular tour participants were:- Geoff, Jacquie, Tony, Sue, Dave and of course me and Moi. We had some wonderfully memorable tours together. Two that immediately stand out, was when Geoff kindly arranged a night at a vegetarian French farmhouse. Moi was a veggie at that time, she's recovered since. The owners took their evening meal with us which was cuss-cuss (aka couscous), however this did not include any flavourings, it was just cuss-cuss, the only taste that we could give it was among the very limited condiments already on the table. On leaving these sparse lodgings, this meal was forever remembered not as cuss-cuss but as shite-shite.

Another memorable two-day stay was at Site de Castel-merle, overlooking the river Vézére, in southern France. It had a series of prehistoric, defensive cave, pathways and steps cut into the cliff face. A very impressive and memorable place.

Stone age caves at Site de Castel-merle,
overlooking the river Vézére, in southern France, 2012.

Our tour around the perimeter of France in 2012 turned out to be our final bike tour. Unfortunately, the mountain passes through the Alps, where the road had unprotected verges with a hundred foot drop just a yard away from the bike tyre proved too much for Moi. The temperature in the low 40s C was not helping, as a result Moi was glad to get home and wasn't planning on any foreign bike trip again. The Wing had to go, and strangely enough, I haven't missed the preparation, and constantly checking every nut and bolt. I very much missed the camaraderie though, and that thrilling moment when we met up and set off on a long trip in a convoy will always stay with me.

Geoff, Tony and myself, Lake Annecy 2008.
Two fine friends sadly no longer with us.

To finish on a very sad note. This photo includes two great mates, Geoff Tailor, Tony Jolly and myself overlooking Lake Annecy in 2008. Geoff seems to be investigating the cause of my deafness.

Both Geoff and Tony continued their motorcycling for many more years, and we socialised on many occasions after Moi and I gave up motorcycling. Unfortunately both Geoff and Tony contracted cancers and died in 2020. Both in their early sixties, very sad, great chaps.

Chapter 23: Bike tours part two, on our own

In "Bike tours part one" I rambled on about touring with friends. Moi and I also toured on our own throughout Britain, Ireland and several countries in Europe. Many of these were visits to WW1 and WW2 sites in northern Europe, and what fascinating places they can be, if you like that sort of thing of course.

There are many areas of interest and to document all would take several volumes. I will attempt to describe some of the images that affected me the most.

The following historical photos were taken at the start of the battle of the Somme, on the morning of the 1st of July 1916. By G. H. Malins, who was the official photographer for the British army. It is an area called the Sunken Lane. The soldiers in this photograph were from the Lancashire fusiliers awaiting their orders to attack the German lines. Geoffrey Herbert Malins was taking crank type moving pictures of the scene, which was, and still is very rare for moving pictures to be taken of soldiers during battle.

A few years ago a lip-reader was employed to discover what they were saying, at first he struggled to understand anything they said because of the very strong Lancashire accent, but after much research he found a way, and what he discovered was mostly profanities. The soldiers had a good idea what was going to happen, and were probably petrified. The Sunken Lane was in fact half way into no-man's land, and the last thing these men would have wanted was someone taking their bloody photos.

The order for them to attack came within fifteen minutes after this photo was taken and all, yes all of them were killed or wounded, some records suggest that all were killed.

The other lush and pleasant photo was taken by me a few years ago from exactly the same spot.

Two very contrasting images of The Sunken Lane. November 1916 and May 2018.

Mr. Malins also took the only images of one of the mines detonated under the German lines, this particular one is named Hawthorn mine, and is approximately three to four hundred yards from the Sunken Lane. This recording shows the first Hawthorn mine detonation at 07.20, which wasn't as successful as hoped. The tunnelling was subsequently opened again and packed with more explosives and then formed one of 19 other mines detonated on the 13th of November 1916. These mines were dug by the British sappers (A combat engineer, a name taken from the French "sappe" meaning spadework). These were miners from Wales and the north of England and men working in the underground and sewage systems of London and Manchester.

These tunnels were up to 90 feet deep and 1,700 feet long, the end of each one was then packed with up to 40 tons of aminol and gun cotton. For various legitimate reasons, two were never detonated. Most of the others were detonated together, killing an estimated 10,000 German soldiers. The explosion was heard in England, and in combination it was the largest explosion in history, and killed more people other than a nuclear explosion. Before the detonation, General Sir Charles Harington remarked "Gentlemen, we may not make history tomorrow, but we shall certainly change the geography".

Hawthorn Ridge mine detonated at 07.20, on the 1st of July 1916

It is difficult to imagine the size of this explosion on a two dimensional image with no relevant reference points. But an observation aircraft flying at 2,500 feet was nearly knocked out of the sky by the chalk debris and shock wave. To give some indication of the size of explosion, the dot on the horizon to the right of the photo is the size of a building. Also the Hawthorne Ridge mine was far from the largest mine detonated during this campaign. The filming of this explosion also resulted in Mr. Malins being knocked off his feet and temporarily rendered unconscious by the shock wave.

In the confusion of war, the two unused mines were never de-commissioned and the whereabouts were lost. One spontaneously detonated during an electrical storm in July 1955, no one was hurt other than a poor unfortunate cow. The other mine is still there somewhere.

The sunken Lane section formed part of the battle of Beaumont Hamel, which in turn formed part of the battle of the Somme. There is a memorial at Beaumont Hamel to the Newfoundland regiment, dominated by a huge caribou.

At that time, Canada formed part of Britain, therefore the Newfoundland regiment was a British regiment. As with all Canadian memorials we visited at that time, the guides are volunteers from Canadian universities, and I believe still are. In this particular section the guide took us from the British trenches, which are still plainly visible, to the German trenches, which appeared to be about 300 yards down a gentle slope across an open field. When we got there and looked back towards the British trenches, the ground appeared to be sloping downhill again. The guide told us that it was a known phenomenon and formed by the lay of the land and an optical illusion.

The guide also told us that the charge on the 1st July 1916, saw many casualties, thousands dead or dying in no-man's-land, and as the battle raged until mid November there was no practical way of retrieving the casualties, so the rotting corpses had to stay where they were for three months.

Not far away is this huge Thiepval memorial, where the names of either 72,337 or 73,412 (depending on source used) soldiers are inscribed who have no known graves.

Tyne Cot near Ypres is the largest Commonwealth grave Memorial, the walls and alcoves overlooking the site contain the names of a further 34,887 soldiers with no known graves, there are also 11,960 graves on the site, 8,370 of these graves contain bodies of unknown soldiers.

The 'Weeping Woman'
one of the sculptures at Vimy Ridge 2009.

The most interesting and artistically impressive memorial is that at Vimy Ridge, this is another Canadian memorial. It was designed by the Canadian sculpture Walter Seymour Allward. It is over 88 feet high and contains 20 sculptures, all of which are beautiful, and look like they could walk away. This memorial contains 11,285 names, of, at that time, soldiers with unknown graves. However, bodies of lost soldiers continue to be found, often buried still in their trenches. Up to date there have been 116 individuals identified that also have their names inscribed on the memorial, but are now known.

They have also reconstructed the British and German trenches in their original position and much of the tunnelling around Vimy Ridge has been cleared. In one section of trenches one could throw a stone between the British and German trenches.

The tunnelling around Vimy Ridge is open to the public. They were originally used to get men and materials up to, and away from the front line, and between trench sections without the enemy noticing. The first time I visited there was an unexploded shell sticking through the roof of the tunnel, it had been there for over 75 years but now sense prevailed and it was removed during recent extensions and opening of more tunnelling.

A 75, year old unexploded shell sticking through the roof section.
What could possibly go wrong?

However, the most moving memorial is that at Menin Gate, Just outside Ypres in Belgium. The memorial straddles the river Kasteelgracht, which was the route all the soldiers took in that area on their way to the Ypres salient. A salient is a bulge in the front line that projects into the enemy territory, it is a vulnerable area as it is surrounded on three sides by the enemy.

Ypres was completely flattened during the fighting, but was re-built entirely just as if nothing had happened in the years following.

Every evening at eight o-clock the police stop the traffic over the bridge and through the memorial, and members of the Ypres fire service play the "Last Post", and what a fine job they do. Depending on the anniversary of that day there are anything up to six buglers. The ceremony is often attended by military personal from all over the world. I have witnessed this ceremony four times, and I am filled with emotion every time.

Crowds reverently observing
while members of the Ypres fire service play the "Last Post",

It is the most moving ceremony, everyone there from all nations respect the sacrifice, and all hats are removed without prompting, there is silence from the onlookers while the Last Post is played. Then ten minutes later the road is opened again for another 24 hours.

Chapter 24: The Huddersfield Narrow Canal

The Huddersfield Narrow Canal runs along the Colne Valley bottom, along with the River Colne and the main railway line from Huddersfield to Manchester.

As a child, I spent many happy times playing in this area. I think humans are naturally drawn to water for pleasure and survival, and boys in particular are naturally drawn to the railway. Huge metal steam engines belching out fire and black smoke, the thrill overshadowing the harm that this black smoke was causing; this became a concern of older people and future generations.

In the late 50s, when my friends and I used to play, go fishing, swim and get up to mischief, the canal was in a semi-derelict state, and all the trade had been taken over by the road and railway. Many of the locks were broken but no-one seemed to care. Some sections had been filled in and buildings erected over the area. The body of water between the lock gates was either high and deep or low and difficult to climb out of if anyone fell into the lock. Large concrete slabs were therefore fitted to the full width of the lock, which formed a shallower watercourse between the lock gates to stop people falling into the deep water by accident or design. But it was still a great place to play.

For centuries, rivers were used for transporting goods; the Fossdyke Navigation was built by the Romans to link Lincoln to the river Trent.

Up to recently, I thought a 'navigation' was a posh word for a canal, when in fact there are subtle differences. A navigation is the re-routing, and/or using of an existing river to form a navigable waterway for goods and traffic. Whereas, a canal is a completely new channel cut into the earth to form the same function.

Before the creation of canals, transporting goods was done on packhorse routes, which were slow, dangerous, unpredictable, and vulnerable. Canals quickly became the solution. Nearly 4,000 miles of inland waterways were built, ultimately forming the backbone of the industrial revolution.

The Exeter Ship Canal was constructed in 1567, but it took a further 200 years for the idea of an inland waterway to develop, these were the Sankey Canal and Bridgewater Canal (near to St Helens and Warrington) in 1757 and 1761 respectively.

The Huddersfield Narrow Canal is the highest canal in Britain. Nineteen and a half miles long, it has 74 locks and navigates over and through the Pennines. Along with the Rochdale Canal, both were built as alternatives to the Leeds and Liverpool Canal. To a British inland waterway enthusiast, Huddersfield's canal is the equivalent to a mountaineer tackling Mount Everest; it is attempted because it's a challenge.

Of course, the biggest obstacle was the Pennines themselves. Work on the canal started in 1794 and work on the tunnel soon followed. However, many unforeseen obstacles were encountered and it eventually took 17 years to complete, at a cost of 50 lives. It took so long to complete that the canals on both sides of the Pennines were completed long before the tunnel, and a packhorse system had to be set up over the top between Marsden and Diggle.

Work on both ends of the tunnel started at the same time. Shafts were dug somewhere in the middle to remove the spoil and the plan was to join them all together.

But difficulties continued. Eventually Thomas Telford, the most renowned civil engineer of that time, was employed to sort things out, in doing so he discovered that the tunnels were not going to meet. The problem was resolved, but as a consequence there were several bends and a height discrepancy, resulting in the tunnel entrance at Marsden being 11 feet deep. This tunnel can boast to being the longest, deepest and highest tunnel in Britain.

Financial restraints and cost cutting meant that there was only one single width tunnel and no towpath. Leggers had to propel the boats through by laying on the top or boards at the side of the boat and propelled by walking it through. Unfortunately, others had the same idea from the other end. Heated conversation and fights often developed in near complete darkness somewhere in the middle. Eventually sense prevailed and a timetable was devised, in turn resulting in a traffic jam at both ends. But at least they were out in the open.

Tunnel End, Marsden, on the Huddersfield Narrow Canal.

This canal was never really profitable. The London and North Eastern Railway ran on the eastern side and parallel to the Pennines. Having previously bought the rights to the canal, they were able to expand the railway system into Lancashire and in turn connect the existing railways systems to the western side of the Pennines, thus connecting Huddersfield, Leeds, Manchester and beyond. As they now owned the rights to the canal they were able to use it by building small connecting sections to remove the spoil from their own tunnelling. First a single-track railway tunnel was completed in 1848. The popularity of the line meant that more capacity was needed; another single-track tunnel was completed in 1871 and another double track opened in 1894.

There continued to be a four-track railway between Huddersfield and Manchester until Dr Richard Beeching decided to axe the railway system in March 1963. Four lines became two and the two single line tunnels were shut, but it was still possible to enter these disused tunnels.

Geological difficulties were discovered during the tunnel construction which resulted in large rock falls and cavities forming. Now weddings and other activities are often held here. Rumour has it that the cavern is sometimes host to pagan rituals with fire, dancing and no doubt chanting and bell ringing. Probably the removal of clothing is also encouraged. I very much hope that they get dressed again before passing through Marsden on their way home.

There are trips for the public through the canal tunnel throughout the summer. The connecting sections and bends are still plainly visible, and there are some very odd sections where the railway line can be seen crossing the roof section of the canal tunnel.

When the canals were first constructed, many areas of industry were connected, and this is how it was in the Colne Valley. However, now that industry has gone, the narrow canal towpath becomes more and more picturesque on the seven-mile walk from Huddersfield to Marsden. A beautiful part of the world; I wouldn't want to live anywhere else.

Chapter 25: Likes, dislikes and how habits change

If we are lucky, we become old enough for our likes, dislikes and habits to change many times. Many of these habits and hobbies change because we have become too mature for the things we loved as children. It is often a good job that we grow out of some of the things that we did as children. If we didn't we would probably find ourselves locked up forever. All too often we hear stories of people (unfortunately, mainly men) who are unwilling or unable to control their immature desires, and of course these people should be locked up forever. Anyway, swiftly moving on.

There were many things I hated when I was a kid. Sprouts, cabbage, getting washed, getting changed and ready in my Sunday best and shopping. I love sprouts and cabbage now, I also slowly began to understand that getting washed occasionally benefited the people around me, and dressing in my Sunday best isn't a chore any more. In fact I like dressing up as described in "Mad 60s biker cured by the love of a woman" in book one, and also in following paragraphs. However, I have never, nor will I ever like shopping.

Moi and I dressing up for a posh choir do 2002.

I have been known to wear a kilt, I am happy to justify this, if justification is necessary, by proudly claiming that I am related to the McInnes/Macinnes family. I have worn it to a Burns night Bolster Moor Malt Whisky Society meeting. Since our resident Scot moved away, I have found myself been volunteered to recite the Burns "Address to a Haggis" poem. I have now done it a number of years and know all eight verses by heart. My English teachers would be proud, although little of it is recognisably English.

The only other classic poem I know by heart is one my big sis Rhondda taught me, it goes.

Eeper weeper chimley sweeper,
Had a wife but couldn't keep her.
Had another, didn't love her.
Up the chimley he did shove her.

They don't write poems like that anymore.

It's actually a nursery rhyme, often used when keeping a skipping rhythm. The subject matter in early nursery rhymes, and what they were supposed to do to children is a whole subject on its own.

One can never get enough dressing up.

The doctor and nurse costume needs little explanation, as I think my expression indicates. I keep it at the top of the dressing up box but it rarely sees the light of day now. I think it must have been a leap year birthday on this occasion.

The one of me in a wetsuit perhaps needs a little more background, it has nothing to do with birthdays, and when I describe the full story, you may understand that it was a good job it had nothing to do with my birthday.

The older we get, the more we find our friends dying around us. Martin Green was another lovely fella and a good friend. Unfortunately, he is no longer with us. Katie and Martin often invited us to stay with them for a few days while they were in their caravan in Abersoch. The photo of that dreaded wetsuit was in that caravan. They also had a speedboat and often went water-skiing. They suggested that I should give it a try. To be more accurate, it was Katie who suggested it, Katie often came up with these strange, mad ideas.

Anyway, they said that the water is quite cold and I would need a wetsuit. As I rarely carried a wetsuit on the bike, it was suggested that I borrow one of Martin's old wetsuits. I am/was six foot tall, and Martin was slightly vertically challenged at around five feet six. Not only that, I think I must have spread out further than Martin, or the wetsuit had shrunk, or more likely both. Anyway, It took me half an hour to get the thing on, periodically having to stop to catch my breath and to calm down following hysterical laughter.

This wetsuit is made of a plastic/rubber material and is in two pieces. There is also a thick strap that goes from the bum area under the bits and fastened to the lower stomach area by two huge press studs to connect the jacket and trousers together, but its main outcome on this day was to push my wedding tackle into places that it hadn't been in before, nor since I'm glad to say.

Every time I tried to stand up straight this bloody strap pushed my bits further up into my intestinal cavity, much to the amusement of the audience of course. I eventually left it flapping down from behind like a set of very strange haemorrhoids, but I didn't care, it was then marginally less agonising.

Off we went water-skiing, I eventually "got up", which was no mean feat, getting my heavy lump of blubber onto the surface of the water while a powerful speedboat was trying to pull my arms out of their sockets.

The cold water numbed the agonising feeling in my lower abdomen, and I eventually found the technique, and I must say I quite enjoyed it.

I was advised that if I wanted a pee, then I should just let go in the suit. I was of course reluctant to pee in someone else's wetsuit, but the space usually taken up by my bladder was greatly reduced by my wedding tackle, so the strain became too much and I did as advised. And what a strange feeling it was. I would describe it as getting into a warm bath arse first. I was marginally surprised that there was still a serviceable outlet pipe somewhere near the outside world that hadn't been permanently corrugated into a useless series of wrinkles. However, the glow didn't last long, and my little fella was corrugated for days afterwards. In fact I don't think it ever regained its previously magnificent dimensions.

I have convinced myself that it is now another skill I will never use again, and yet another opportunity to say "The older I get, the better I was".

I was going to ramble on about getting ready to go out when I was a kid, and the other hate that has never gone away, and that is shopping, but I'll leave that for another day. Like many of my rambles, they start with a theme in my head, and then within a couple of lines they shoot off in another direction. Quite fascinating sometimes how they take on a life of their own.

Chapter 26: Music in Yorkshire

When my little brother visits us in sunny Huddersfield with his family, he favours renting a local house or cottage. During a family celebration in early December 2021, he rented a house in Golcar, and insisted that it was the house that our maternal grandparents Edward and Maggie Holdsworth lived in during their final few years. Realising that Nick was quite young at the time, and the coincidence was stretching the likelihood to its limit, I doubted that he was correct. It turned out that it was indeed the same house. I had to visit of course to reminisce, and discovered to my joy that little had changed. New fittings, but essentially the same layout. That visit immediately evoked many happy memories: the constant smell of new-baked bread, and granddad showing me how to play cards and encouraging me to sing, which he did with all his children and grandchildren.

One of the memories I and all my cousins have is the organ in the corner of the lounge. To be more accurate, it was a harmonium. Invented by Alexandre-Francois Debainin the mid 1800s, it became the instrument of choice for those who wanted to pro-duce a church organ sound in smaller venues like music rooms and private homes. There were even portable varieties for playing outside.

All three of his daughters sang in choirs for much of their lives, and Frank played in brass bands up to the final evening of his life, described in 'Uncles in the war' ramble. All of them lovely people, of whom I am very lucky to have very fond memories. Unfortunately, all now gone – but not forgotten.

*Granddad Holdsworth performing in Gilbert and Sullivan's
'Pirates of Penzance' in about 1910.*

Granddad Edward Holdsworth – "Ted 'o' Jims", his nickname around Gowca – was a very skilled amateur musician. He was choirmaster at one of our local chapels, and organist at another. This was when all chapels, churches and schools had their own choirs and an organ or piano accompanist. Many villages and large factories had brass bands. There was music everywhere. Huddersfield still maintains a great tradition of producing music of all kinds and from many cultures.

Vibrant and varied. Yorkshire brass bands are the envy of the world: Black Dyke, Brighouse and Rastrick, Grimethorpe Colliery and Sellers bands to name but four, all proudly part of Yorkshire. Grimethorpe Colliery Band featured in the 1996 film 'Brassed Off'. However, in the film they were called Grimley Band.

Choir music also features greatly in our Yorkshire traditions. Huddersfield Choral Society, Opera North based in Leeds, Colne Valley Male Voice Choir, and Yorkshire Bach Choir from York are but a very small number picked from an endlessly larger number of highly skilled and entertaining musicians performing the more traditional classical music.

In addition, there are wonderful examples all across our county of Asian and far eastern music and dance groups, as well as pipe bands, and the very recently popular ukulele groups.

Over the years, traditions build, many for reasons lost in history. The first of the two choir traditions in this part of the world is to be found at the end of the first line in Cym Rhondda, where in the line 'Guide me o thou great redeemer', we replace redeemer with 'Jehovah'. The second tradition, relevant to the winter Christian festivals, dictates that we should only sing 'Christians Awake' on Christmas Day itself. Traditions of our forbears should be respected, if not necessarily adhered to. I have been known to sing 'Christians Awake' at other times as well, but don't tell anybody. It is, after all, a great rousing carol, and, like Cym Rhondda, a song that you can really get your teeth into.

One of my favourite kinds of music from outside our shores is that of the Steel Band. These bands started from very humble beginnings in Trinidad, where young, industrious and talented lads made use of the oil drums left by the USA military following WW2, to provide music during their Mardi Gras. The family of a steel band could be as many as six different sections from bass through to tenor, and they are all called pans.

As well as having many talented individual music teachers, we have at least two music collages in Huddersfield that are second to none outside London: Huddersfield University and Musica Kirklees. Thom Meredith is the principal of the latter and also the musical director and conductor of Colne Valley Male Voice Choir. During my time with this choir, featured in the 'choir' ramble, I found Thom to be an all-round fine fella, who luckily has the patience of Job.

Thom Meredith conducting a massed Kirklees schools' choir,
at the McAlpine Stadium, Huddersfield, during the millennium year celebrations.
He is wearing a union flag waistcoat designed and sewn by Moi's fair hand.

Huddersfield boasted many venues favoured by very famous musicians, a tradition that continues in the wonderful Huddersfield Town Hall. Other venues are no longer with us but at one time provided entertainment worthy of note, for example, on 29 November 1963, the ABC Cinema (The Ritz).

Along with an estimated 70% of the British public who claim to have seen the Beatles live, Moi actually did. Aged 14, she camped out all night on the pavement, along with her older school friend and dozens more Beatles fans. Moi told me that at least one very friendly and helpful police officer stayed with them all night to ensure their wellbeing.

They never heard a note from the stage, but had a great time. By November 1963, the Beatles didn't need to be heard; just the fact that they were there, jiggling about a bit on the stage in person was exciting enough for the fans. It certainly was for Moi and her mate.

Another notable event took place on Christmas Day 1977, at Ivanhoe's in Huddersfield. This was the final time The Sex Pistols appeared together in Britain. In my humble opinion, if there was no sound from the stage on that occasion, I'm sure it would have been an improvement, although I wasn't there – and could not have been paid enough to attend. 'It takes all sorts', 'Nowt so queer as folk', and any number of other clichés one might wish to use!

Chapter 27: More tours by motorcycle, this time to Poland

From the 1980s up to 2012, Moi and I travelled to many countries around Europe on our various motorcycles. We used 11 different British ports, some on several occasions, and coincidentally toured through 11 different countries of Europe – many of those several times. In 2008, we rode to Żagań in western Poland, a place with family connections, and once again experienced the pleasures and challenges of a continental road trip.

If our planned tours were to start in northern Europe, we usually sailed from Hull to either Rotterdam or Zeebrugge. Rotterdam is the largest port outside Asia, and didn't we know it. There is port activity and equipment for miles and miles.

Zeebrugge is part of the Belgian city of Bruges, hence the name, which means 'Bruges at sea'. On one trip, we stayed in Bruges for a few days and encountered a creature that was a blood-sucking, flying, biting thing that lives in the canals, and that is where they should stay. Two of these little buggers had a chunk out of me that took two years to fully heal. Fortunately, most of our encounters with Europe's inhabitants were much more pleasant than that.

On our trip to Poland, we broke the journey by staying in Helmstedt, northern Germany. Just next to the hotel was a steak house. My expectations were raised, knowing that the Germans are very much into meat. I like my steaks rare, but knowing that some of our continental neighbours assume that us Brits like our steak 'crozzled' (over cooked) to within an inch of its life, I was a little concerned that I was going to have trouble with getting my steak the way I wanted it.

The waitress, although very helpful and friendly, could speak just as much English as I could German. When I asked for my 'blue' steak, she frowned and shrugged and then said, "Ah, the English way". I assumed at this point that it was all going belly up, however, when it came, it was among the best I have ever had. We did the same on our return a week later, and it was just the same – perfect.

The German autobahn is an interesting and exciting experience, particularly for riders of a powerful motorcycle. There are no speed restrictions, and everybody seems to be happy travelling at 80 to 100 miles an hour. On occasions we may feel like opening up and find ourselves travelling at 120mph when someone/something comes flying past at another 50mph faster.

Somehow this never felt dangerous. Everybody seemed to be aware of what speeds others were doing, and there was no bullying or weaving in and out. Everybody just patiently waited till it was clear then lit the afterburners.

In fact, I have found European drivers much safer and more helpful in general than those in Britain. I suspect that this is at least partly because of the space available on the continent. Wagon drivers will notice that you are waiting to pass and give a wave through when they can see that the coast is clear. This takes a little getting used to, particularly on a motorcycle, but we soon discovered that they were trustworthy and helpful.

There may be an argument here to suggest that faster speeds make us more aware. I have always maintained that riding a motorcycle makes us into better drivers (if, unfortunately, not necessarily into good drivers). As motorcycle riders, we are vulnerable and so we learn to be very aware of our surroundings, a skill we take into our car driving. Unfortunately, motorcycling is risky, and many of the people who ride motorcycles also like to expand the risks factor. This of course is part of the fun and thrill of motorcycling. I took many risks, I'm not trying to justify it, it's just the way we/I was made. I blame testosterone. It has a lot to answer for.

One disconcerting habit they seem to have on the continent, which I haven't witnessed in Britain, is when the continentals are delivering a new tractor/cab front section of an articulated wagon, they tow it backwards, so when I was happily driving on the inside (right) lane I would see in the distance a wagon apparently driving straight for me but was actually travelling in the other direction. That was something that I never got used to!

Routes 2, 10 and 12 across Germany took us into Poland, where the road becomes the E30. This is the road that Hitler constructed to take his army east into Poland and then into northern Russia, and in 2008 it still consisted of the original concrete slabs while we were travelling east. The contrast between this road and the autobahn was huge. Each slab of about 20 metres had over the years settled and each section was a different height from the last and the next, which meant our best speeds were around 40mph and even that was uncomfortable. Luckily, they had constructed and recently widened the road to create a dual carriageway, meaning the journey was much more comfortable on our return.

On our trips to Poland, we have found it to be a very special place. We noticed how disciplined everyone was. One small example of this is how people cross the road. Everyone would use a regulation crossing point, the equivalent to our zebra or pelican crossings, and then quite happily wait for the green 'go' sign before stepping out into the road, even when there was no traffic to be seen, and possibly hadn't been seen for some time.

People are also extremely kind and helpful. In a previous tour in 2008, Marian, one of the local Żagań historians, kindly helped us for three days to try find traces of our great-grandmother. One of the most impressive images of that area was the tidiness of the graveyards, which I can only assume is typical.

In one particular graveyard, there were over two and a half thousand graves, all very neat, clean and tidy, many with little boxes in which to keep gardening tools. Another example, I think, of the Polish discipline

A typical example of a very tidy Zagan graveyard

A further incident of Polish helpfulness above and beyond occurred during the same stay in Żagań. Moi bought something (as she does) that turned out to be too big for our luggage space. I took it to the local post office with a hope of getting it posted back to Blighty.

Even though I had attempted to learn a little Polish, I found nothing in the language that I could get any clues from. French, German and Spanish all have many similarities to English, whereas Polish has nothing, therefore I entered that post office with nothing but pointing and grunting as clues to what I wanted. Even though nobody in the post office could speak English, two of the staff must have felt it a worthy challenge to walk me through it.

The item was a length of cloth bought from the same mill that great granddad had worked at in the late 1800s. The two very helpful ladies found a box and wrapped it up. I wrote the label and paid.

2012 saw our final long motorcycle tour. Our age, the constant checking of the bike and my own riding standards were becoming as much of a chore as a pleasure. However, my interest in all things military continued, and in 2018, Moi, our daughter Rachel and I booked a coach tour to northern France and Belgium with Leger Battlefield Tours, a coach company specialising in touring battlefields, as the name implies. What an excellent and informative week that was.

Chapter 28: Krakow and Auschwitz-Birkenau

Of all the WW1 and WW2 sites I have visited, I had never plucked up the courage to visit a WW2 concentration camp. One evening during that WW1 battlefield tour, I suggested that we visit Auschwitz. Moi could not face the idea, saying that she has heard enough about it and that was plenty. I could not argue of course, but Rachel and I agreed that it is something everyone should do if they could.

We duly booked a flight to Krakow in November of 2019. Krakow is a beautiful city, it has a central market square reminiscent of many towns and cities on the continent, where we could, and did, sit outside the many bars, cafes and restaurants around the square and just watch the world go by while sampling some of their culinary dishes, and of course, one or two of their many famous vodkas.

I would also recommend a visit to the Wawel Royal Castle. There are many castles on the continent. Unlike Britain, our continental neighbours do not have the luxury of being surrounded, and therefore protected by the sea. Each country and city in Europe had to build castles for protection. Poland is in an unfortunate geographical location, right in the buffer zone of Western and Eastern Europe, and has been subjected to a thousand years of upheaval, just one of which was WW2.

The name "Poland" derives from the land of the Polans (open planes, or grassland). They were an old Slavic tribe.

Wieliczka Salt Mines are near Krakow and also a fascinating place. Extracting salt from brine and then rock salt has been carried out there for hundreds of years. Vast caverns have been cut in the rock. Many of these caverns have been turned into places of religious pilgrimage.

Wieliczka Salt Mines near Krakow.

Nearly everything in this image is cut from rock salt, even the huge chandeliers.

A build up to the holocaust can be found in the Oskar Schindler's enamel factory on the outskirts of the city. Oskar Schindler employed many skilled Jewish workers at his factory, and he needed these workers to continue his business. In his official capacity as a loyal party member, and a considerable amount of bravery, he persuaded the local authorities to allow him to continue employing a Jewish workforce. As a result, directly or by accident, he managed to save hundreds of his Jewish workers from a fate that six million other Jews were not.

Since the fame of the film Schindler's List 1993, the factory is now a museum, much of which is dedicated to Krakow under Nazi occupation.

The following photo is of a notice issued in December 1941, offering a reward for "denouncing a Jew wandering unauthorised around the district". The reward was the equivalent to a couple of bottles of vodka, or a few packs of cigarettes.

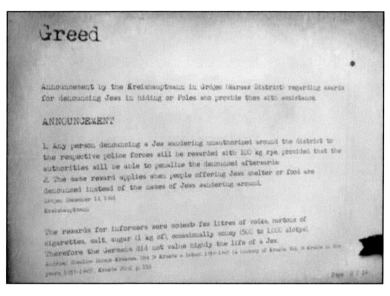

A reward notice for denouncing a Jew 1941.

Many, if not all of the Jews in the Krakow ghetto eventually found themselves in Auschwitz-Birkenau. This now brings us to the reason we visited Krakow

Auschwitz-Birkenau is in fact several camps, dedicated to different functions. Auschwitz was originally a WW1 army camp in the district of Oświęcim in southern Poland. Following the

German invasion of Poland in 1939, they set up a political prison camp in the old army barracks and changed the name to Auschwitz. A name that evokes a chill in the human soul.

Following the German invasion of the Soviet Union in 1941, Auschwitz was then used as a prisoner of war camp and also where the first gassing of Soviet prisoners was carried out.

The iconic image over the gate to Auschwitz with the words
ARBEIT MACHT FREI, (work sets you free).

Most of the buildings in the Auschwitz camp were of a substantial two-story brick construction. Built by the prisoners of course, all heavy labour in and around the camp was carried out by prisoners. There were over thirty of these blocks in total, used, among other things as barracks for the SS (Schutzstaffel) guards, (a German fanatical protection squad), and also housing the local Gestapo headquarters. These building were also used for administration, prison, hospital, early gas chambers, crematorium and a brothel.

Among the first gas chambers were in Auschwitz. Hundreds of prisoners were packed in by the SS guards, and Zyklon B dropped through the ceiling. It is also where the first ovens were used to dispose of the bodies.

The notorious block 11, quickly dubbed the "death block". Knowing what went on in the building it isn't surprising that it was called "death block". It was mainly used as a gaol (jail) for prisoners from the camps who had been accused of clandestine activities, attempting escape, organising mutinies and maintaining contact with the outside world. Also people from the surrounding villages who were accused of helping the prisoners were also tried here. If they were lucky, those that were not immediately shot on discovery found themselves tried, found guilty by the summary court and then shot in the courtyard between block 10 and 11.

However, for the most unfortunate the sentencing may include various forms of torture, including starving to death, hung by the arms behind their backs, experimentation on how long it took them to die by injecting different chemicals, or incarceration in a two foot square brick box not quite big enough to stand up in, having first been forced to crawl through a small opening at the bottom that was then securely fastened by a metal door. They were in complete darkness until they went mad and died. They also carried out experiments with Zyklon B, in preparation for the much larger extermination system at Birkenau.

In an area where death was everywhere, block 11, has a place of its own.

There are other blocks almost as notorious. The so-called hospital was in fact occasionally used to treat the sick or injured, but if it was one of the prisoners then they had to recover fully and quickly or their usefulness was ended.

Other experiments on Jewish women were carried out in the hospital, experiments on different forms of sterilisation by Prof. Dr. Carl Clauberg and Horst Schumann. If the victim (patient) survived the treatment, they were likely to be killed so that a post mortem could be carried out.

Dr. Josef Mengele also worked at this camp, experimenting on twins, giants, dwarfism and Romas. The twins were nearly exclusively children, and if one of the twins died, then the other would likely be killed also.

Drs Clauberg, Schumann and Mengele all survived the war. In fact many of the scientists and doctors who had previously worked for the Nazis and the SS were employed by the allies after the war so they could pass on their vast knowledge of death.

One of the brick blocks just inside the main gate at Auschwitz was a brothel. It is difficult to understand with our modern sensitivities, but this was one of the activities that gave a fair chance of survival. The ladies would not have their hair cut off and were allowed to keep their own clothing. They were fed comparatively well and had regular medical checks. Each of their rooms had a small hole in the door so that the guards could ensure that no harm would befall them. The main reason for their survival was the fact that they were working indoors.

A toilet block.

This is one of the toilet blocks. They could only be used at certain times of the day, and usually only once a day. Ten minutes were given for maybe a thousand people waiting for an opportunity to use 150 toilets, therefore it was very lucky if they got one hole to themselves, more likely to be two or even three people to a hole. Strangely, the cleaning out of the toilets was another of the desirable jobs, because it was also one of the survivable indoor jobs.

Auschwitz to Birkanau railway.

This is the section of railway that took people from Auschwitz to Birkanau. Each side of the track was where 372 wooden building were situated. Each one was about fifteen metres wide by fifty metres long. They looked like large chicken coops. Many had 300, or more triple bunk beds. The most favoured one was the top bunk. The living conditions, the diet and health of the inmates was such that their bodily functions were unpredictable, and being on top meant that you were not going to get somcone else's bodily fluids.

The pecking order in these huts, and in the work details were often dictated by the most vicious and ruthless. Kapos was the name given to those assigned from within the prisoner's by the SS to keep order. The men and women were kept separate. There were men and women Kapos assigned to their respective barracks. The reason for this separation was to limit the chance of pregnancy. Any prisoner caught fraternising without permission would very likely be shot immediately.

As the Kapos were selected from within the prisoners themselves, they were likely to be hated more than the SS guards, and were sometimes killed by the other prisoners. Another function given to other prisoners was that of a Sonderkommando. These were special units employed to burn the bodies in any of the four crematoriums or in the open air. They were not allocated to do any killing. That was the job of the SS.

In the book 'The Boy Who Followed His Father Into Auschwitz' by Jeremy Dronsfield, published in 2019. He stated "that there was mistrust and hostility between the Polish Jews and the German Jews". No doubt both felt the same about the Soviet Jews. Also nobody cared about the Romas (Gypsies), the disabled, Communists, prisoners of war (usually Soviet) and criminals. All this was of course fuelled and encouraged by the SS guards, divide and conquer, the SS were very good at this. They may have been fanatical, psychopathic, murderous killers, but they were not fools.

This may have something to do with why it needed so few armed guards to keep order. There is an argument to suggest that some of the ethnic groups thought that the Germans were doing the right thing, until it was their turn of course, and then it was too late. "Hate destroys the hater" a quote from the Henry Norman book "Real" 1897.

Documentary evidence seems to show that the number of SS guards in 1941 was around 700, rising to over 2,000 in 1942. The number of SS guards in the Auschwitz-Birkenau camps rose to 4,500 during the evacuation in 1944 just before the Soviet's liberated the camps. It is much more difficult to ascertain the number of prisoners at any one time, as thousands were being killed to make room for the latest arrivals. And thousands went immediately to their deaths on arrival. One estimate put the number of people killed in the gas chambers at an average of 600 per day, and many were dying from mistreatment and disease. However, a reasonable guess can be carried out. Of the 372 wooden sheds constructed at Birkenau, at least 300, were used as prison cells, 1,000 in each shed means approximately 300,000 prisoners for the SS guards to control under normal circumstances. Many of the SS personnel were doctors, architects and administration staff, therefore the number actually guarding the prisoners was much less. Taking into account that they were on shift duties, days off and leave, there were between a quarter and a third of the available SS guards actually guarding the prisoners at any one time.

Thousands of political prisoners, ethnic groups and gypsys thought to be particularly undesirable by the Nazi regime were deliberately worked to death on hard labour duties outside digging pits and drainage channels, constructing the buildings and railways, and used as slave labour in local factories. All those who were unlucky enough to be allocated any of the outside duties were unlikely to survive.

The most favourable job within the camp was in Canada. This name was given to the thirty sheds allocated to sorting the belongings of all the new arrivals. The name Canada was used because it was thought to be a land of plenty. At its height there were 2,000 people working in Canada. As in the brothel, all the workers in Canada could wear their own clothing, or take better clothing from the luggage that they were sorting. There was also plenty of food to be found among the luggage. All valuables were meant for shipping to Germany. However, some found their way into a pocket along the way. Some items were hidden away by the prisoners and used as bribes or on the black market.

The arrival of just one trainload,
probably heading straight for the gas chambers in the distance.

This is a rare photo of new arrivals, all the possessions that they are carrying would by processed in Canada, and all these people would also be processed for their usefulness, but most, if not all would have gone straight to their deaths. All the people in this photograph appear to be walking towards the gas chambers, two of which can be seen on the horizon. The Birkenau gas chambers were working from June 1943, to November 1944. From late summer of 1944, every trainload similar to the photograph above went straight to the gas chambers. Then each cattle truck was then filled by the Canada workers with the possessions of previous occupants to be sent back to Germany.

I have read that some extermination camps had a gravel road that led to their gas chambers, and these were periodically raked to find discarded valuables thrown away by the new arrivals rather than have them found by the guards or Kapo's.

Shoes collected in just the last few days before liberation.

In the museum section of Auschwitz, there are rooms displaying a huge pile of shoes, luggage, spectacles, pots and pans, and hundreds of prosthetic limbs similar in size to the mound of shoes in the photo. There is also a section showing a mound of human hair, big enough to fill a medium sized van. We were asked not to photograph this out of respect, so of course, I didn't. The most shocking aspect of these photographs is that all that is on display was collected in the last few days before the German's left.

During the tour we were taken to what remains of the gas chamber and crematorium of Birkenau 3. Demolished by the SS in their attempt to cover their tracks. There were four in total but this was the only one we were shown on the tour.

Just before the Soviets arrived to liberated Auschwitz-Birkenau, in January 1945, the Germans tried to destroy all the evidence that this was a mass extermination camp. They also set fire to many of the timber building in Birkenau, leaving just hundreds of brick chimneystacks as an eerie reminder of their past. Although much of the timber not destroyed by the Germans was taken by the locals after the war for their own use.

As the Soviet liberators were approaching in late 1944, any prisoners able to walk were force marched west towards Germany, leaving a small contingent of guards ordered to shoot the 7,000 prisoners who were too ill to leave, and destroy all documentary evidence, but the guards thought better of it and left before the Soviet's arrived.

Even after all this, the ordeal of many of the prisoners was not yet over. Before Rachel and I visited Auschwitz-Birkenou, I prepared myself for the traumatic moments by reading books and watching documentaries. The best and most informative book I read was 'Auschwitz' by Laurence Rees, 2005. There were several notable first-hand accounts describing their attempts to return to their own homes after being liberated.

Walter Fried returned to his hometown of Topolcany in Slovakia. Before the war, his family owned a restaurant, but when Walter returned he soon found that the family apartment and the restaurant were now occupied by people placed there by the

Soviets. Fearing what was happening, his father had left some gold, jewellery and money with a Christian friend and neighbour, but on his return Walter was told by the neighbour that they knew nothing of it.

Helena Citronova, and her sister were trying to find their way home from Berlin where they had been taken during the evacuation of Auschwitz-Birkenau. As they sheltered each night in abandoned buildings with other refugees, she described the Red Army as acting like conquerors rather than liberators, and she witnessed many drunken Red Army soldiers taking whatever they wanted, including the women and girls. Helena had one lucky escape when a Soviet soldier attacked her and was asking if she was German. Had she not shown him her camp tattoo, she felt that he surely would have raped her. Helena and her sister had previously been robbed by a group of Soviet soldiers leaving them with even less than they had, which, of course, was virtually nothing.

Tatiana Nanieva had worked as a nurse in her hometown in western Russia when the Germans captured that area in 1942. She witnessed many of her friends being raped by the Germans. After the camp was liberated in 1945, Stalin had announced that there were no Soviet prisoners of war, only traitors of the Soviet Union. For her 'crime' of allowing herself to be captured by the German army, Tatiana was sentenced to six years in the Gulag and a lifetime exile in Siberia.

Red Army soldiers took their vengeance. It is impossible to ascertain an accurate number of assaults, theft, rape and murder carried out by the Soviet 'liberators' but it must have been in the hundreds of thousands.

There is a very poignant quote from the book. "But the revelation that women who had already endured so much mistreatment in camps like Auschwitz were then subsequently raped by their liberators adds a level of nausea to the history that did not exist before".

Immediately following hostilities, it became obvious that vengeance was not the sole speciality of the Soviet Red Army.

There is the site where the first, and later to return, commandant of the camp, SS-Obersturmbannfuhrer (Lieutenant Colonel) Rudolf Höss, was tried by the Polish courts and hanged on April 1947. The vengeance aspect of this was that this hanging took place within sight of the palatial house on the camp grounds that he apparently happily shared with his wife Hedwig and their five children.

After the war, many Jews found themselves stateless, homeless and lost. Luckily the state of Israel was formed in May 1948, so at least some could at last find some peace of sorts.

Who of us would honestly say how we would act given the same situation and conditions? Would we do anything to survive? Would we fight back and if we were about to die at least try to take a guard with us? Would we do as millions had done, capitulate and surrender to our inevitable fate? Or would we do as many did and commit suicide? Or if we had Nazi sympathies, of which there were many in Europe at that time, would we dutifully carry out our orders?

There was only one documented, serious rebellion in Auschwitz -Birkenau. Over time prisoners were able to make contact with the local partisans, also small but regular amounts of explosives were smuggled into the camp by the slave workers from the camp who worked in the local factories each day. Enough explosives had been smuggled in so that In October 1944 Sonderkommanda from crematorium 4 were able to completely destroy the building, and attacked the SS guards and Kapo's, killing three and injuring about a dozen more. Of the prisoners who survived the initial attack, two hundred more were rounded up, and shot. In total 451 Sonderkommandas were killed that day, but their brave effort meant that the capacity to kill within the next 2/3 months was significantly reduced, and a countless number of prisoners unknowingly survived, possibly thousands, owing to the heroic efforts of those 451.

Luckily, very luckily, we live in a beautiful country where we are not likely to be put to these tests. However, I'm sure many thought that in Germany in the early 1930s.

The Devil has visited mankind on many occasions. He lived at Auschwitz-Birkenau.

I have never understood why the Jews have been hated. It all seems to have started by the killing of Jesus, and the Jews have been blamed for it. This of course was a long time ago, and how we are able to judge the conditions and laws that brought this about cannot be fully understood now. There may be some jealousy involved that has helped continue this hatred. The Jewish population seems to have a reputation of having good business sense. Many of the stories from survivors of the Holocaust seem to suggest that they were academics and professionals, owned shops or factories. I would have thought that this is a good thing, but it seems we do not all think the same.

Chapter 29: Childhood procedures soothed by jelly and ice cream

As regular readers of my rambles will know, I tend to ramble to and fro on different subjects that interest me, and one train of thought often leads me on to quite a different one, as I think the title 'Norky's Ramblings' would suggest. I also, much to the consternation of my friends and family of a more delicate disposition, am happy to describe my medical interventions and procedures in some detail, as I did in 'Surgical adventures with the wedding tackle'. Reminiscing about childhood procedures leads me to recall stories – medical and otherwise – told by my mother, which reminds me of the wrath of another mother, my aunt, after an incident involving a cousin, a grandma and a bottle of Drambuie.

For many children, any time spent in hospital can be traumatic and therefore memorable. I was no exception. I was circumcised at 18 months old and had a tonsillectomy at three years old. I have a very vivid memory of looking through the bars of a cot in a room full of other cots and beds, and being given jelly and ice cream by a lady in a white coat, which must have been special because I remember enjoying it. I'm sure that would have been when I had my tonsils removed. I can't imagine ice cream soothing the discomfort following a circumcision.

Mum would occasionally talk to me about my own bits and pieces, which always made me feel uncomfortable. More than once she would explain why I had been subjected to the circumcision but never explained why I was being subjected to the explanation.

How babies grew inside the mother was another favourite subject for our medical chats, but she never approached the subject of what happened before that. This particular detail was something I had to stumble across in the fullness of time. I think it's fair to say that I've been stumbling ever since.

My brother has also been circumcised, so I suspect it's an example of a fashionable operation of the time. Other fashionable operations over the years have been the removal of knee cartilages, hysterectomies and more recently, caesarean sections.

Along with the circumcision, Nick was also persuaded to have a knee cartilage removed when he was approximately 20 years old. I think I can safely say he has not had a hysterectomy or a caesarean section yet, although he did become a father in 2021, when he was 64 years old – but I'm fairly certain it was a natural birth. Joking aside, I cannot imagine looking after a six-year-old daughter at 70 years old and not being able to hand her back to someone else at the end of the day. Having said all that, the few times I've seen them all together, he does seem to be taking to the task very well. Good on 'im.

Mum didn't just chat about medical matters. I was more than happy to listen to her describing anything really. She never read to me, as books didn't play a large part in our general household. However, my sister Rhondda read quite a number of children's books. I remember her trying to get me to read one of Enid Blyton's Famous Five books, but there were hardly any pictures in it, so that didn't last long, a good effort on Rhondda's part though.

Mum would sit with me and tell me stories and encourage me to help her with some household chores usually carried out in those days by the lady of the household: cooking, baking, sewing, knitting and darning. I was always happy to give it a go, as long as I wasn't expected to do it all the time. I also carried out other tasks usually associated then with the gentleman of the house, like making tools and boys' toys out of scrap wood, gardening and car repairs with Dad.

One of Mum's stories that I still remember was the one about 'The grass is greener on the other side'. This story fitted nicely into the deep and narrow Colne Valley. The story goes something like this. A young lad called Peter asked his mum one morning why windows on a house on the other side of the valley were golden, so his mum suggested that he should go over there and find out. It took young Peter all day to walk over to the other side, but no golden window could he find.

Disappointed, he turned to walk back and as he did, he noticed as if by magic that the windows on his own house were golden.

The Drambuie story. One of my cousins got themselves into lots of trouble with their mum when we all attended the 1958/59 New Year's Eve party at Grandma and Granddad Holdsworth's.

Like many women of her generation, Grandma Holdsworth had never set foot in a pub and was indeed a life-long teetotaller. For some reason best known to them, my cousin brought a half bottle of Drambuie to Grandma and Granddad's party. Either Grandma spotted the bottle and asked what it was, or it was offered to Grandma as a taster.

Grandma, bless 'er, wasn't wearing her glasses and misread the label and said "It must be alright – it's for babies".

Grandma Holdsworth, 1967.

It is unknown how she came to that conclusion; she possibly thought it was some kind of gripe-water. Anyway, the offending relation didn't think it was the right moment to enlighten the innocent and allowed things to develop. Grandma asked for a tumbler full – of possibly the only alcohol she had ever consumed – and it was dutifully provided. Luckily, there were no ill effects and Grandma was even heard to say "Eee, that's very nice".

My cousin has never admitted that it was done deliberately; I don't think they even admitted it to themselves, but they did get into hot water afterwards with their mum.

Chapter 30: Cost of living in 1947, jammin' an' things on t' telly

In the year that I was born, the population of the United Kingdom was just over 50 million, the average price of a three bedroom house (if you could get one) was £2,200, average income for men £6 8s 0d (£6.40) and women was £3 9s 4d (£3.47). The difference is surprising and quite shocking really. Women earned just over half of what the men earned for full-time work. A postage stamp would cost three old pence, approximately one and a half new pence now. One gallon of petrol cost two shillings and four pence, approximately 12p in new money. A loaf of bread was one shilling (5p). Postage stamps seem to have inflated the least of all household items with an approximately forty-fold increase. Petrol, housing and particularly wages have had a 100 to 200-fold increase in just over 60 years.

The other day I was jamming with my mate Roger. Jamming is when friends get together to perform music for their own entertainment without an audience; sounds a bit like jazz. (Sorry, jazz fans – only joking!) a bit.

As we were jamming, we started to reminisce about some of the early pop music programmes and game shows on television. Moi joined in and between us we could remember many, and even remembered some of the presenters and performers.

In recording our memories below, I am fully aware that I am inviting corrective feedback from someone who knows far more than me, as happened following my suggestion in my previous ramble in the Yorkshire Bylines magazine entitled 'Puberty' book one. I had the cheek to suggest that a particular play could have been broadcast on either BBC or ITV in 1957. The reader's response was detailed in the extreme.

It was pointed out that it could not have been ITV, as I had suggested, as we could not pick up the signal in our area at that time. I was informed of the date and name of the transmission mast that was erected to cover our area; and fine details of the 'hertz and megascrotes' it used, or something like that. He (I can only assume it was a he) attempted to identify what the play I was describing could have been. Many more details were included, much of which I didn't understand.

I imagine the same chap will be searching through his piles of old 'Radio Times' stored in his back bedroom for the correct versions of our collective and aging memories listed below. We should admire the dedication of these people, perhaps!

Six Five Special was the BBC's first tentative, reluctant advance into pop music in February 1957. The hosts were Pete Murray and Josephine Douglas. Apparently, it was the job of Josephine Douglas to interpret Murray's jive talk for the older viewers. All male presenters on early television were always smartly dressed in lounge suits, if not in dinner jackets, and all the women were usually in some version of a ball gown. It's difficult to imagine a scene where a woman in a ball gown is interpreting 'jive talk' from a chap in a lounge suit.

The programme started with the song "Over the points, over the points, over the points, the six five special steaming down the line" performed by Don Lang. This and the visual background of steam trains encouraged the idea that the programme title was something to do with a steam train timetable; in fact, it derived its name from the television transmission timeslot of 6.05 in the evening. A time between the afternoon children's television and the more adult entertainment later in the evening, 6–7pm was dubbed 'toddlers' truce'. This was the hour that the government broadcasting department had decided was a fitting time for toddlers to be put to bed. Governmental attempts at controlling our daily lives isn't a new thing.

Pop music on television really kicked off in the 60s. In 1961, we had *Thank Your Lucky Stars,* hosted by Brian Matthew, Pete Murray, and Janice Nicholls. *Ready Steady Go* from 1963 was hosted by the very lovely Cathy McGowan and ... somebody else (opening for the reader memory here, although I never cared who the other person was, Cathy McGowan took all my attention). Both were produced by ITV/ABC. The BBC were late, as ever, at grasping the pop music nettle, but in 1964 they produced *Top of the Pops*, which proved to be the most lasting of these types of pop music programmes. Although they hardly ever performed live, singers and players mimed to their latest songs, some better than others, all too often hampered by the artists not being able to hear what was actually being broadcast.

Janice Nicholls had first appeared on a pop panel program called Juke Box Jury, produced by ATV in 1961, where a panel, chaired by David Jacobs, was asked to score a latest pop song out of a possible five. One of the panellists was picked from the general public. Janice was an attractive young woman from Birmingham, and when she said "Oi'll give it foive" in her Birmingham accent – in the days when strong regional accents were rarely heard on television – she became an instant celebrity. A record called '*I'll Give It Five*' was produced on the Decca label. Like most records that are trying to cash in on some sort of fad, it was rubbish of course.

Nearly all, if not all of the early presenters on the BBC had middle England plum accents, and many were chosen because they had titles or some connection with aristocracy. Lady Isobel Barnett springs to my mind, a regular panellist on '*What's My Line*', a show where the panel had to discover the occupation of a guest member of the public by asking questions with only a yes/no answer. If the panel discovered the correct answer before three 'no' answers from the contestant, then they were declared the winners of that round. Riveting entertainment. This may sound like sarcasm, and of course it is looking at it from our more modern world. But entertainment was much simpler and in many ways more innocent, and "What's My Line" was in fact essential watching.

Another very popular programme was the game show *Take Your Pick* hosted by Michael Miles. This was the first British game show to offer cash prizes. First broadcast on ITV in 1955, it had actually started on Radio Luxembourg in 1952.

This show had what was called a "Yes/No Interlude", where Michael Miles asked questions to contestants picked from the audience. The challenge was to avoid using the words 'yes' or 'no' to the questions put to the contestant by Michael Miles – hours of fun. Just to build the pressure even more a member of the production team called Bob Danvers Walker stood at the side of the petrified contestant with a dinner gong, which was struck at any yes or no, further adding to the terror. If anyone managed a whole minute without answering yes or no, Mr Miles reluctantly gave them a half crown – 2s/6p, twelve and a half pence now.

Entertainment was much simpler, more innocent and cheaper in those days. They were equally frugal with spending on set design and probably borrowed the gong from the boarding house next to the studio.

Another very popular game show with the same humble beginnings on Radio Luxembourg was *'Double Your Money'* hosted by Hughie Green. I recently watched an episode of *Double Your Money* on-line (I'm a bit sad like that sometimes). For £16 the contestant was asked to name all ten provinces of Canada! They had to earn their prize money in those days. Even if it was fixed, and it probably was, most people, I'm sure, would be hard pressed to remember the answer to that question even if they had been told it beforehand.

I can't remember what I had for my dinner two hours ago, but I can remember the name 'Bob Danvers Walker' from the early sixties. Memory is a funny thing. I look forward to hearing from my friend with all the proper information when he has searched through his *Radio Times*.

A Yorkshire couple had just won the Euro Millions and were contemplating what to do next. The wife said, 'What shall we do about the begging letters?' and he said, 'Keep sending em'.

Chapter 31: The big screen and family fallouts

My father's youngest sibling Trevor became a cinema manager at the Picture House and Essoldo cinemas in the centre of Huddersfield, both now gone of course. Even the street where the Picture House was situated has now gone, replaced by a shopping centre. The Essoldo cinema building is still there – due to be transformed into Huddersfield Arts and Heritage centre, but not a cinema I'll be bound.

I have always been fascinated and entertained by the big screen, ever since my big sis Rhondda took me, first to Slaithwaite and then to Golcar cinemas when I was too young to go on my own. The Slawit cinema was originally named the 'New Theatre' but later was known as 'The Winston' after Winston Churchill. I was sure the Gowca cinema was called The Picture House' but apparently it was called The Ritz. I later went with friends to the matinee at another Picture House, this time in Milnsbridge to watch Roy Rogers, Flash Gordon, The Lone Ranger, Marx Brothers and many more. Milnsbridge (Brig) and Gowca cinemas were about half a mile apart and would not have had the same name, but this would have been how it became confused in my tiny mind and fading memory.

At one time during our return home to our council estate after a Saturday afternoon matinee, we passed through a recreation ground with the normal swings, roundabout, see-saw and slide. We noticed a lad – one of the older boys – called David stood on the top of the slide on the outside edge of the safety railings, shouting at the top of his voice to all that would listen, "Look, I'm

Superman!". He was obviously inspired by what we had all watched that afternoon. Unfortunately, David, who was not blessed with much wit at the best of times, must have also been influenced by the flickering lights, for he then launched himself into the air. Luckily he landed with a thud on his head, which broke his fall, his only meaningful injury was a broken arm.

After a little while, I started venturing to the Huddersfield cinemas on my own, to Uncle Trevor's cinemas in particular, because he would let me in for free. I remember watching Dr. No, one of the early James Bond films. I was on my own at this particular time. I had just settled into the film when Uncle Trevor found me out in the darkness and asked how old I was. I told him but also explained that I had seen the film the previous week, which was true. Uncle Trevor said, "Very well you can stay". I was 14 years old at the time.

I'm sure Uncle Trevor was very concerned that I may have been corrupted by all the shocking goings on in Dr. No. Mind you, watching Ursula Andress striding from the surf would be enough to corrupt any mere mortal 14-year-old. In about 2005, Ursula Andress sold the bikini that she wore in the film and admitted that she received more money for it than she was given for her part in the film.

One of my favourite characters in these afternoon matinees was The Lone Ranger (played by Clayton Moore). His sidekick Tonto knew all the survival skills necessary to keep The Lone Ranger out of trouble; in fact, if it hadn't been for Tonto, The Lone Ranger wouldn't have lasted five minutes.

My big Sis Rhondda subscribed to a weekly (I think) magazine called 'Cinema' or 'Illustrated Cinema'. In this magazine, we could send for a photograph of our favourite film actors. I begged, bribed and cajoled her to send for a picture of Tonto for me, which she duly did. I had to give her priority on our favourite chair for a whole week and boy, did she take advantage! Even when she was late for her date, she would insist that I vacate the chair just so she could sit in it for thirty seconds. Older sisters are like that sometimes.

A week later, the photo duly arrived, and to my lifelong disappointment, it wasn't a photo of Tonto wearing his native leathers and feathers – it was a photo of a fella in a suit and tie. This was Jay Silverheels, the actor who played Tonto. This was probably my first realisation that actors were normal people in real life, which of course was very disappointing.

The Curzon cinema was located in the centre of Huddersfield between the bus station and the technical collage which I was attending at the time. As I was passing I noticed that they were showing a Brigitte Bardot film. I had heard of and seen quite a few erotic and revealing photos of this actress. Temptation got the better of me. I thought lusting in a darkened cinema was much more entertaining than learning more about algebra, or something else just as useful in my job as a textile apprentice carding engineer. As the lights dimmed the pensive anticipation reached fever pitch. I soon learned that the film was in black and white and subtitled. I left after ten minutes. Algebra would have been just as entertaining.

Sibling rivalry and jealousy has happened forever, and can be quite aggressive at times. Over the generations, I have witnessed many family fallings-out. Thinking of Uncle Trevor reminds me of my first experience of this – Aunty Marlene.

Marlene was Uncle Trevor's wife. To my young eyes, Aunty Marlene looked exotically foreign, possibly Italian. I thought she and/or some of her family were also Roman Catholic, which was another difference for me.

In 1961, Marlene alienated herself from my family when my parents didn't ask her daughter Beverley to be a bridesmaid for my sister Rhondda. Uncle Trevor came to Rhondda's wedding alone. Marlene kept away from us forever after that. I was 14 years old and that was my first experience of how over-reacting can influence our judgment forever.

In 2012, over 50 years after the falling-out with my parents who had been gone for over 15 and 20 years respectively, I phoned Marlene for a chat and to get some birth dates for my family tree. She was reluctant to enter into any meaningful conversation and refused to give me any family details. Her excuse was that she had never got on with the Norcliffe's, even though she apparently had a loving marriage with one. I was fourteen years old at the time of Rhondda's wedding and of course had nothing to do with any arrangements, this didn't seem to make any difference, I was a Norcliffe apparently, but as far as I know she still uses her married name, and both her children are or were Norcliffes. She's still around and well into her nineties, but I haven't spoken to her since 2012.

I still struggle to understand these attitudes. I cannot imagine what my siblings Rhondda and Nick would have to do for me to fall out with them forever. It's fairly easy to fall out when we're kids and know nothing, particularly when one is a boisterous younger brother to a bossy older sister, but forever is a long time. If anyone is in this situation and reading this, please think about how long forever is and make that phone call. I can guarantee that there will be a huge weight lifted off your shoulders.

Uncle Trevor
alone at Rhondda's wedding
December 1961.

Lightening up a little.

Albert Hargreaves, a rural country farmer from Barnsley in Yorkshire, was mourning the death of his favourite sheepdog. After digging deep under his mattress for some spare cash, he visited the local jeweller, and said:

"Nah then lad, sithi ear, I want thee to do mi a solid gold statue of mi favrit dog Lassie thanose".

"Certainly" said the jeweller, "would you like it eighteen carat?"

Albert replied, "Nah tha daft bugga, just have it chewin' a bone".

Chapter 32: A WARTS walk to St Aidan's

Walkers And Ramblers Tenacious Stalwarts W.A.R.T.S.

We few, we happy few, we band of brothers, sisters, wives, ex-wives, ex-husbands and occasional daughter and father. The WARTS walking group: wonderful friends one and all.

This photo was taken on one of our many walks, and was taken during a walk to St Aidan's RSPB nature reserve near Castleford.

St Aidan's reserve is a fascinating area. It was once an opencast coal mine (a sunshine mine, dug from the surface, not through shafts dug into the ground). The River Aire and the Aire and Calder Navigation once ran side by side and along the edge of this vast mine. One night in March 1988, due to previous deep mine subsidence, the banks of the river Aire broke, allowing the whole of the river between Castleford and Leeds to flood into the mine. Over the next four days, an estimated 3.7 million gallons of water left the river, and at one time the river Aire flowed backwards, in effect uphill, until the mine filled. Luckily, it all happened overnight and no one was injured. It resulted in a 250-acre lake nearly 250 feet deep. The Aire and Calder Navigation survived but was then very vulnerable. An act of parliament was needed to divert the river and canal, and for the next few years, work was carried out to re-route almost three miles of both the river and canal 200 yards further south, creating a single new navigation.

Work was then started on pumping all the water back into the river. In 1998, the mine re-opened, but only produced coal for a few more years, and in 2002 the mine was closed altogether. It was then allowed to flood again, and in 2013 it became an RSPB nature reserve.

This section of the Aire and Calder Navigation is a very pleasant area for walkers. The new Lemonroyd Lock was built during the re-routing work, and close by is a steel, box-section, bench that must be the most uncomfortable, fully functioning bench in the country. Every time we visit this area, we have to remind ourselves how uncomfortable it is. I'm sure the bloody thing fights back.

St Aidan's is a wonderful place both for twitchers (bird watchers) and just for walking aimlessly along the seven and a half miles of footpaths.

During its time as an open cast mine, a monster 1,200-ton drag-line excavator was used, and it's still there as a permanent exhibit. Nicknamed 'Oddball', it was manufactured in the US in the late 40s and shipped to Britain during the Marshall Plan of the early 50s. It was at that time the largest excavator in Europe

Oddball.

This is Oddball. The large oblong structure on the right is approximately 100-feet long and 50-feet high and wide. It's the size of a small aircraft hangar.

The bucket is big enough to drive a car into and capable of scraping 25 tons of earth or coal with every bucket load. Oddball could actually walk on its huge feet, but only backwards and at about 0.2 miles an hour, about the same speed as a tortoise at full gallop. Although I don't think a tortoise can walk backwards at all. Could be wrong again – I await further education from a learned zoologist or 'vetnry'.

The Marshall Plan was similar to the earlier 'Lend-Lease' system, whereby the US sold, loaned or gave goods, food and material to many countries around the world to aid the fight during WW2 or the recovery from it afterwards. This system, and the fact that the US was not attacked or invaded on its mainland, meant that it was unimpeded in retaining, indeed vastly increasing, its manufacturing capacity and productivity. This went a long way towards ensuring the US's position as a superpower.

One of the small but significant changes made in Britain during the Marshall Plan was in farming. Before the war, much of the heavy lifting and pulling on farms was done by the horse. Under the Marshall Plan, thousands of tractors (mostly second-hand, I believe) were sent from the US, each able to do the work of several horses, but more quickly and much more efficiently – and a tractor didn't get tired. Many of the soldiers had learned new mechanical skills necessary for modern warfare and the transferring of these skills onto the tractor and other agricultural work was fairly straightforward.

We carry out our walks on Tuesdays, Fridays and Sundays. The Tuesday walk tends to be about 10 miles, whereas the others are shorter, but all will include a café. We have become connoisseurs of the café, favouring the ones that provide banter and conversation, and of course good grub. The ones that try a gimmick often fail. Trying to be posh by serving food on dods 'a' wood (a wooden plate) never works for me; Internet and game cafés don't do it either. However, the proprietor who enters into some banter and/or abuse definitely cuts the mustard. One such is in the centre of Castleford, first visited after our walk around to St Aidan's. On entering, we immediately noticed a wallpaper border running all around the café with every type of coffee known to man proudly printed on it.

Our corporal was excited, for he is picky about his coffee. He asked for 'A flat white, please'. The salt-of-the-earth local lass looked at him with a glare that could kill at twenty paces and said through gritted teeth, 'We do white coffee and we do black coffee'. The corporal meekly pointed at the wallpaper border. She must have been impressed by his bravery, or more likely felt sorry for him, and actually entered into conversation. But it didn't last long. It went something like, 'I've been here five years and you are only the second person to ask that'. She didn't go on to explain what happened to the first, but she seemed to forgive the corporal after an acceptable period of grovelling and cowering under the table.

Another notable café is in the Todmorden area. On our first visit to this establishment, the owner was just shutting but as there were five of us, she asked us in and locked the door. It was more like a deli shop than a café, but the fine lass provided chairs, coffees and the biggest slab of the best hot quiche I have ever had. She quickly ascertained that we had two doctors in our party that day and must have thought it fitting to describe her time as a health visitor in Leeds.

One of her regular visits was to a brothel. It may be a surprise for some to know that there is a brothel in Leeds, possibly even more than one. It may be even more surprising to learn that the local council employed someone to check on their wellbeing.

Anyway, she went on to describe one of her first visits. The madam asked her if she wanted a cuppa, and then shouted in a madam sort of tone 'GEORGE! TEA'. Eventually, in shuffled a gentleman carrying a tray of tea and biscuits, completely naked save for a frilly pinny.

Our friend showed surprise, so the madam explained 'Oh! that's nothing. We have a chap who comes here, that following an appropriate degree of disrobing and preparations are carried out, asks for clogs (supplied presumably) to be tied to certain part of his anatomy, and then he crawls around deliberately making a clip-clop sound on the floor with his clogs'.

Not for me, thank you very much, give me a good hot Quiche Lorraine any day.

It seems to be a domination, ridicule or humiliation thing. I have an image in my mind that these gentlemen were reincarnations of two of my ex teachers. I have to say, I enjoy that image a lot.

There were other stories equally unsuitable for delicate ears but if we bump into you on one of our walks, and if you're of a sound disposition, we will be easily persuaded to share them with you. Hopefully of course, you can join in with inappropriate and unsuitable stories of your own.

Chapter 33: How Yorkshire helped to shape the modern world

A pile of abandoned millstones set me thinking about inventions and inventors and about the achievements of notable Yorkshire men and women.

Abandoned millstones. Overlooking Hathersage, Sheffield.

The other day I was allowing my mind to wander, as it does …

Sorry, where was I ………? Oh yes! I was going to tell you I'd been thinking back to a moorland and quarry walk we WARTS walking group carried out overlooking Hathersage just west of Sheffield. There were dozens of abandoned millstones just lying where they'd been left, presumably after the need for millstones had passed. You could have one, if you asked nicely and had a bloody big wheelbarrow and a couple of stout lads to help.

After recalling these millstones on the moors, I allowed my mind to wander further, as it does……..sorry, where was I this time? Oh, yes! I had begun to think of inventions and notable people that had shaped our world and, in particular, shaped our world in Yorkshire.

We could say that the wheel had the greatest influence in progressing humankind's ability to transport things. Not wheels like the ones in the photo above of course – it would take a hell of a big horse to pull four of those on each corner of a cart. I of course mean normal wheels, probably starting with a log, then cutting a slice off a bigger log and fastening it to the end of the smaller log, and so it began. I might also humbly suggest that it wasn't the wheel that was the most influential invention, but the second wheel.

The control of fire and water was of course a huge benefit to our wellbeing. Fire developed naturally through volcanic eruptions and lightning. But the control of water as a power source required human intervention. It was harnessing the power of rivers – a fairly modern development – that drove the waterwheels that powered many types of mills, including the mills using the millstones in the photo above.

Humans then went on to develop the technology to build relatively safe dams for reliable year-round drinking water. They also fed canals which, together with the controlled creation and harnessing of steam, went a long way to making the industrial revolution possible. I would argue that string, yarn and rope were greatly influential as well. The development of methods for extracting long hemp and flax plant fibres enabled the production of strong and durable string, rope, sacking and linen cloth (see Matthew Murray in the list of notable people below). Also, flax made excellent bowstrings, which in turn made Henry V and King Harold very famous.

Yorkshiremen and women have had a key role to play in shaping our political history, with two notable prime ministers. Herbert Henry Asquith, prime minister from 1908-16, was born in Morley, while Harold Wilson, in office from 1964-70 and from 1974-76, was from Huddersfield.

William Wilberforce 1759–1833, a Yorkshire MP from Kingston Upon Hull, was a pioneer and the leader of the movement to abolish slavery. He was able to see it become law a few days before his death.

Betty Boothroyd, born in Dewsbury, broke ground for female MPs in 1992 by becoming the first woman to be elected Speaker of the House of Commons.

Guy Fawkes, born in York, did his best to change the country's politics in 1605, but came to a very sticky end. After a lengthy period of torture, he was sentenced to be hung, drawn and quartered. Disappointingly for the judiciary of the time, he died early as the sentencing was being carried out, but they continued anyway. They had to make sure he didn't do it again.

Flamborough Head saw England's first lighthouse in 1669.

As mentioned above, Matthew Murray's factory in Leeds pioneered machinery for separating flax fibres and manufactured parts for the first steam locomotive in 1790.

Harry Brearley of Sheffield invented 'stainless steel' in 1913. Sheffield also saw the first kickerball club – Sheffield FC, formed in 1857. More importantly, of course, in 1895 Rugby League began life in the George Hotel Huddersfield. Folklore suggests that William Webb Ellis 'picked up the ball and ran'

During a kickerball game, thus inventing the game of rugby, though in fact several forms of rugby had been around long before kickerball.

Percy Shaw of Halifax patented the 'cat's eye', a very important road safety device, in 1934.

And, of course, Yorkshire pudding; invented by angels sent from the heavens to show just the deserving people of Yorkshire how to make the best puddings in the world.

Perhaps most famous of the Yorkshire writers, the Bronte sisters, Charlotte, Emily and Anne, and their brother Branwell were born in Thornton, later becoming associated with Haworth. Past poet laureate Ted Hughes (1930-98) was from Mytholmroyd. The current holder of the post, Simon Armitage, was born in Huddersfield.

While his creator Bram Stoker was Irish, Dracula first set foot in Whitby in 1890. Daniel's Defoe's Robinson Crusoe set sail from Kingston upon Hull.

The county has produced a host of other notable characters, for example Captain James Cook FRS (1728–79) explorer, navigator, and cartographer – born in Marton, near Middlesbrough. Kingston upon Hull saw the birth in 1903 of the famous aviator Amy Johnson, while the first European woman in space, Helen Sharman, was born in Sheffield.

Remembered for somewhat less glorious reasons, Yorkshire woman 'Old Wife Green' was the last witch to be burned in England, an event that took place in Pocklington in 1630. Perhaps, as with the ducking stool test for suspected witches, the locals were watching to see whether she survived – which would have confirmed that she was a witch – or not – somewhat belated proof that she wasn't.

Finally, we should mention Barry Cryer 1935–2022, born in Leeds. A very funny fella. Apparently, and more importantly, a pleasant chap to boot. RIP. This is one of his:

A Yorkshire lad was celebrating his diamond wedding anniversary and was describing to his friend the secret to a long marriage. He claimed it was the fact that they had nothing in common that kept them together, and they argued about everything, upon which his wife said, "No we don't".

Chapter 34: Memories and thoughts following another W.A.R.T.S. walk.

One of the members of the WARTS walking group was previously nicknamed 'Lieutenant', a further addition to all the other names earned during his time at a private school, or while he worked as an undercover tax inspector at a nunnery (filthy habit). Now he prefers to be called 'The Forager', as he has an interest in horticulture and knows things about living off the land.

He will often point out a fungus growing in a pile of something and say, "That's edible" (we have to assume he is pointing at the fungus). To prove his confidence, he has even taken some home and prepared what he claims is a spectacular culinary dish fit for a king, although his wife doesn't have the same confidence, and neither does anyone else as far as I am aware.

Probably poisonous. 'sulphur tuft'

If, like The Forager's wife, you said, "I'm not gonna eat that", then you would feel much better than if you did, for this is sulphur tuft, and it would make you very, very ill in five to six hours. However, probably not terminal, maybe.

As previously described in the WARTS ramble, book one, he has also sold his soul to Zeus, the God of Clouds, as it never rains if he is with us on our walks.

As if control over the weather and his immunity to toxins isn't enough, The Forager will send all members a walk report including interesting history of the mills, railways, houses and paths we came across that day, and it may also include Ordinance Survey (OS) maps and an online description.

One example was in February 2022. We were passing Longwood Beck, a tributary to the River Colne. A section to this beck meanders in a very strange way, forming a very tight figure S. It looked so unnatural that we speculated that this area must have had in its past some building forcing its course. Sure enough, Forager found an old OS map and the history of Hirst's Mill on that site.

Longwood Beck (large stream) now meanders through very pleasant countryside and into Longwood Compensation Reservoir which called 'Woh Carr' when we were kids. According to a water board chap I was in conversation with, Woh Carr is the oldest reservoir in Huddersfield. It once fed many mills further down Longwood and Milnsbridge, but feeds nothing now. It just sits there looking pretty.

Hirst's Mill was a very early example of a scribbling mill. Scribbling or carding is the part of the textile process which straightens, combs and separates the fibres just before spinning and then weaving. By the early 1800s, methods of spinning and weaving and associated machinery had been evolving for some time, but carding was still painstakingly done by hand. Necessity being the mother of invention, the carding machine eventually came along.

One section of a carding machine.
Photo with kind permission of Lightowlers Yarns, Meltham.

The photo is just one section of a modern carding/scribbling machine, but the principle remains unchanged. The process starts at the hopper end – this particular machine has four carding sections, the original carding machine developed in the 1830s, had only one – the carding process then finishes at the condenser, which provides slubbing ready for spinning. Unlike the 1960s when I worked in't mill, and at any time before that, there are safety guards everywhere now.

It was a large machine, each section being approximately ten feet long and seven feet high, and there could be several sections to it. As a result, it could not easily form part of the spinning and weaving cottage industry of earlier generations. A purpose-constructed mill became the answer. Eventually, many machines together with associated processes were brought under one roof. Dams in the rivers or becks were constructed to ensure a constant and reliable water supply for the waterwheels, and later for the steam boilers. Hirst's Mill had a 25-feet-diameter waterwheel. All that remains of the mill now is the overgrown cobbled access road and bridge.

Another link that The Forager sent was to the Underground Histories website of Alan Brooke. Part of this lists Huddersfield mills from 1790 to 1914. Entry number 178, Lees Mill, Golcar reads as follows:

"1858 HC 20 Nov: John Taylor's four year old son drowns in goit, resuscitated by Mr Dean, surgeon. Finds on arrival that the old method of applying sod of earth to child's face and nose had been tried."

Of course, there are more questions than there are answers available to this tragic event. Presumably "resuscitation" didn't mean that the poor child recovered as I think it would mean now. What was the "old method of applying sod of earth to child's face and nose" supposed to do?

The one thing I can answer is what a 'goit' is. A weir was constructed across the closest river or large watercourse to form a kind of dam. A valve opening was built into the upstream body of water which allowed water to enter a channel, very much like a small canal, which ran into a larger dam constructed in a convenient area near the mill. The channel is called a 'goit'.

The goit between The River Colne and Low Westwood Upper Mill.

The photo shows the beginning of a goit fed by the weir on the River Colne in the background. This particular goit sits between the River Colne and the Huddersfield Narrow Canal. It runs approximately 320 yards from the river and fed Low Westwood Upper Mill, now derelict but still defiantly hanging on by its fingertips.

This is by no means the longest human-constructed goit, or artificial watercourse. The Catchwater feeding Blackmoorfoot Reservoir just outside Huddersfield is over two kilometres long (although there was no such thing as a kilometre when it was built in the 1870s).

A giggle interlude.

A very careful Yorkshire farmer from Selby takes his dog to the vets, and says, "Na-then vetnry, mi dog's swoled a condom thanoze. Can thee do awt'?

"Leave it with me and come back in a couple of hours", said the vet.

Half an hour later the farmer rings the vet and says, "Don't worry about the condom lad, mi wife's found another in't medsin cabinet".

Chapter 35: Be proud of your Accents

During our walking group's rambles, we often bump into people who are prepared to stop and enter into conversation, probably for the same reason as we do – that is, we're all glad of the breather, particularly halfway up a steep hill, of which there are many in our neck of the woods.

We bumped into a woman the other day, I would say of about 50 years old. During our conversation, I asked her if I could detect an Irish lilt in her accent. She immediately apologised saying, "I've lived in Huddersfield for 30 years and still have my Belfast accent".

I insisted that she shouldn't apologise, not only because the Irish accent is very pleasing on the ear, but also because our accents partly define who we are, and we should all be proud of our roots.

There have been times when people tried to cover their humble beginnings by developing a middle England accent, particularly in politics, teaching, university posts, the BBC and the higher echelons of the military. Of course, efforts should be made to make ourselves understood, and I think to an extent, we all do that: we speak in a certain way in our own home and within our family environment but express ourselves differently elsewhere. Even so, in my humble opinion, we must proudly keep our basic accents.

I have never lived outside Huddersfield, nor can I speak a foreign language. English has always been more than difficult enough for me. Therefore, I cannot distinguish the subtle differences in the regional accents in a foreign language, but there must be few other languages with as many differences in accents and dialects in such a small area as there are in Britain.

If we were to magically invent a time machine and go back to, say Shakespeare's time, 16th-17th century, we could tell them a thing or two about the dramatic events that were coming their way.

They would be interested to hear of the imminent gunpowder plot in 1605 during the reign of King James 1. We would explain how distrust of the monarchy during this period would culminate in Charles 1 being tried for treason and executed in 1649. We would describe the glorious revolution of 1688, the act of union 1707 and the continued conflict with our nearest and dearest European neighbour, France, until a battle near a small town called Waterloo in 1815.

We would recount the horrors of the slave trade and its abolition in 1833, as well as the two world wars of 1914–1918 and 1939–1945. One thing that would surprise them the most would be the formation of the Welfare State in 1945 and the NHS in 1948, where the government and others of power and influence were willing (I suspect begrudgingly in some cases) to help the poor and needy. Sending people to the moon in 1969 and bringing them all back.

Well, we could tell them all these things and more, if only we could make ourselves understood. The sounds of English have changed so much in the intervening years that understanding each other would be a challenge. It helps to explain why many of Shakespeare's jokes fall flat for us – they rely on puns and rhymes to words that no longer sound the same.

Imagine what it would be like even now for a Londoner to suddenly find themselves in a local pub at closing time in say Glasgow, Hartlepool or indeed in the centre of God's country, Barnsley. It's very likely that they wouldn't be able to understand a word – just what it would have been like for us everywhere in the 16th century. It would be English, of course, or a version of it. Except perhaps in Glasgow. I'm never certain what language they speak there. Of all the accents that I encounter, the Glaswegian accent is my most troublesome.

As a nation, we are the richer for it. Doubtless, the good folk of Glasgow, with their rich and colourful accent have things to say that deserve our full respect, if only we could understand them. I'm sure they do it on purpose.

Go to anywhere in God's country and seek out an old farmer and attempt to start a conversation – that is, if you can get past the first comment from him, which could be "Gerroff mi land or I'll set mi dogs on ya", which I'm glad to say is getting less likely these days. But if you get as far as a conversation, you'll discover many variations of the Yorkshire accent, and that's just in one county, but as we all know it is a vast area of hills, valleys, moors, lakes and a coast, from boroughs of tiny quiet hamlets to busy bustling cities.

I'm proud to be from Yorkshire, and proud of my accent, and so should everybody, no matter where they're from. After all, they can't help being born outside Yorkshire.

The Green, Marsden c1940.

The Green beside the River Colne in Marsden. The little bridge in the background is often mistaken as a packhorse bridge, when in fact it was constructed for the vicar to get from the vicarage behind the trees on the right to the church behind the trees on the left.

Giggle time again.

In 1975, Uncle Ronnie emigrated to the USA. My dad and Uncle Ronnie were fanatical Yorkshire cricket supporters. One day, Dad had to send his brother some sad news, which he did in the following telegram:

REGRETS DAD DIED THIS MORNING STOP FUNERAL WEDNESDAY STOP YORKSHIRE 360 FOR 6 STOP BOYCOTT NOT OUT 105 STOP

Chapter 36: Community service and home-front support

Describes some of my interesting experiences as a community service volunteer – brought to an end when I was needed to help as a dad.

In a previous ramble entitled Inappropriate, Antisocial, Illegal Behaviour, I mentioned that in early June 2014, I joined the community voluntary service. Not only was I one of the marshals at the Tour de France cycle race, I often found myself being volunteered to help out on the police information stalls or handing out leaflets in targeted areas of police concerns. I had also volunteered six times for role-playing at the West Yorkshire Police training academy near Bradford. This also was a fascinating insight into police training. I carried out role-playing in scenarios such as abusive husband, care home manager, white supremacist, a witness in a bar fight or a grumpy neighbour. Each team carrying out one of the scenarios and two trainee police officers arrived to deal with your particular role-play and we were encouraged to act out our roles in any way we thought fit, without being violent, of course. The violent acting during the bar fight was carried out between the trainers and the trainees, but I thought it was very tame, and I'm sure they would have learnt more on a rugby pitch.

There was also a surprising opportunity for me to learn something about myself.

During the white supremacist scenario, I was to complain to the police about my house being vandalised and I had a good idea who it was. I was encouraged to be as abusive as possible and when the first few pairs of trainees turned up with their respective trainers, I entered the role of an abusive racist, with a view to intimidating the police cadets.

I was able to enter the acting role quite well I thought, until one pair turned up with what appeared to be an Asian supervisor/ trainer, and I found myself unable to use the racist language that I had been using for most of the day. I mentioned my hesitance to the trainer as they were leaving and his reaction was probably predictable. He said, "You should have done mate, I get it all the time".

Another interesting variation of human nature became apparent during the abusive husband scenario. I had been locked out of my home and I was to try to gain access in an aggressive and noisy manner. Some trainees had me in handcuffs as soon as I opened my mouth, while others allowed me to wander off and hide, so then they had to find me.

I would have thought that domestic violence is a very common problem that the police have to deal with and putting the aggressive perpetrator immediately in handcuffs would have been my default position. But I suspect that the training had suggested a softer approach. What I know for sure is that handcuffs are very uncomfortable, though I suspect mine were 'snugly' fitted following the trouble of having to search for me in my hiding place.

In 2016, I volunteered on the water station for the world triathlon championships in Leeds. It was quite warm that day, and during the amateur event the competitors gathered around and even queued, desperately gasping for water which we were able to hand out in pre-filled paper cups.

For the elite professional event run later in the day, we could only remove the tops from 50cl plastic water bottles from trustworthy bottled water suppliers. We had to place them on the palm of our outstretched hand and were told not to move. During the cycling, no one came near us, but during the final running stage they all came to our side of the road. Not everyone took a bottle, and we had no hint when they were going to take one either. They all ran past so fast that the only clue that we got was a strong bang on the hand, after which the bottle had vanished.

In 2017, I resigned from the community voluntary service. Interesting jobs were becoming scarce and I was being squeezed out by sociology students, police volunteers and police community support officers who wanted the experience for their education or to get more involved with regular policing. Which was fair enough; I just did it for my own entertainment and was quite happy to step aside.

I had other priorities in any case. Just at that time my daughter Rachel had developed what was potentially a serious medical condition. She was also going through the final stages of very lengthy and difficult separation and found herself solely responsible for selling her house, all this required us to pull together and needed our undivided attention.

During her recovery, she stayed with us for 11 weeks, two days, and six and a half hours or so, while she was fattened up by Moi and gently trained up by me. She responded very well and moved to her new flat in Bailiff Bridge in mid December. However, that move was a bit of a nightmare, too much stuff crammed into too little space. We were constantly moving stuff to get space for other bits of bloody stuff. I'm going on holiday if she moves again. I began singing a little song while I was there, very much to Rachel's annoyance (part of the fun really) it went something like, "Shift, shift, shifting stuff, shifting stuff again, shift, shift shifting stuff, shifting stuff again", to the tune "Row, row, row your boat gently down the stream, merrily, merrily, merrily, merrily, life is but a dream".

Rachel and I had our DNA tested during her stay in 2017. We were both over 50 percent Scandinavian, with a lot of Scottish, Irish and Welsh included, as one would imagine. We both also had a significant percentage of Iberian, Italian and Eastern European. Both of us are 100 percent European. My wife Moi then decided to have her own DNA test.

She had boasted on many occasions that her great-great-grandfather was Scandinavian, immigrated to Hartlepool from Sweden to work in the dockyard, and married a local 'Monkey Hanger' lass. Therefore, we all expected that her Scandinavian roots were going to match or better Rachel's and mine. It turned out that she had none, and even more surprising, there was a small percentage of Nigerian and North African. Moi thinks it will have been the Romans who brought the African DNA to England. Truth is, we will never know, but very interesting all the same. To a degree, best off not knowing.

The Monkey Hangers of Hartlepool story goes back to the Napoleonic wars, a French galleon was shipwrecked off the coast of Hartlepool. The only survivor was a monkey dressed in a French uniform, presumably to amuse the French crew. The locals couldn't get the monkey to answer any of their questions, so, never having seen a monkey or a Frenchman before, they quite understandably thought it was a spy and hung it.

Chapter 37: Danger ramble

Reminiscing about life as a youngster getting up to mischief: wild swimming, playing on railway lines, and trespassing!

Described in a previous ramble entitled 'Construction sets and playing with fire' again in book one, the playing with fire aspect of our boyish entertainment was far from the only potentially dangerous pastime we indulged in. As previously mentioned, as soon as our mothers were confident that we were able to find our way home, we were all encouraged to play out. I had the added incentive that not only was it home, but it was also where I was fed.

There were many boys and girls of all ages to play with on Bolster Moor, and later on the Sycamore Avenue estate. All happily forming little groups and gangs, usually somewhere near our own age groups. There were occasional little scraps to establish, or re-establish, a pecking order. But I can't remember anything serious. The scraps were usually between best mates, and we were still best mates a few days later when tempers had calmed.

A budding Bradley Wiggins in 1957. His legs were never as magnificent as these fine specimens, surely.

Many of the dangers we faced were self-inflicted, of course, thanks to the challenges of our environment. When the Colne and, our neighbour, the Holme valleys were formed towards the end of the last ice age, about 15,000 years ago – long before even I was born – vast amounts of ice and the rock that the ice had penetrated broke away and gauged out the valleys that we see here today. Also, later in our stumble through evolution, many stone quarries were dug to provide material for reservoirs, roads, walls, farmsteads and houses. As a consequence, there were many cliff and quarry faces to climb and test our nerve.

Even though, as described by Sir Isaac Newton 1643–1727, gravity is the weakest of the four fundamental forces, it still hurt a lot when gravity proved stronger than the grip we had on the rock face or the tree branch. It's usually the sudden stop at the bottom that causes the most serious injuries, but being young, we usually bounced, but cuts, bruises and broken arms and ankles did occur.

Wild swimming: hazardous, potentially deadly – in other words, fun. Water was another natural hazard we couldn't resist.

In the Golcar area, Woh Carr (its real name is Longwood Compensation Reservoir) was our nearest reservoir big enough for us to swim and/or fish in. We spent many a happy time near the footbridge fishing for roach, perch and pike. The other end of the 'rez', adjacent to the dam wall, is where we swam. This, of course, is where the water was deepest and coldest, only one of which we knew to be a problem before health and safety was invented. Even the simplest minded amongst us knew that if we submerged ourselves over our heads then our health could suffer. That knowledge didn't stop some testing the boundaries of survival in the interest of bravado and daring. Boys will be boys.

Another of our popular swimming areas was the canal in Milnsbridge. This was an area of concentrated textile mills and there was one section of the then unused canal that was always warm due to the finishing and scouring outlets adjacent to the canal. This again was before health and safety, and we knew nothing of the harm we could suffer as a result of whatever the water from the mill might contain; nor did we know anything about Weil's disease, also known as Leptospirosis, caused by a bacterium carried by animals, mostly rats and cows, which is not uncommon in canals. If we had ever heard of it, we wouldn't have gone anywhere near the place.

The Huddersfield narrow canal had other temptations for the most foolhardy (which is mostly the male of the species of course). The locks on this canal were only 6 feet 10 inches wide and who could resist jumping it, if they wanted to, or if you hadn't got to get back home just then for your tea, or if we just didn't have a bad leg that day.

The railway was always a fascinating area to explore. The Colne valley boasted four lines before Dr Beeching drew a pencil line through two of them. There always seemed to be goods trains, usually coal, with their locos belching out black smoke while they struggled up the gradient of the valley. We would dare ourselves to stand directly over the relevant line on the open girder footbridge while a train passed only a few inches below us, excitement as it approached proving too much sometimes. This footbridge was called Nancy Bridge, it was the most convenient route for us to get to the canal and railway. It has now been replaced with a tall closed sided box section footbridge, we can't even see over it now, never mind through it.

Another excitement was for someone to generously donate an 'aipny' (half penny) to a very worthwhile experiment of placing it on the track and see how big it became when the train had passed. We were always fascinated that the aipny had nearly doubled in size similar to the dimensions of a penny. Somebody would eventually speculate that they could pass it off as a full penny, usually the lad that had originally donated it.

Not only is trespassing on the railway stupid and dangerous, it is also illegal. It's one of only a very few areas where trespass is not a civil matter but criminal, and therefore the police could and should be involved. Otherwise, in this beautiful country of ours, the sign on private land saying "Trespassers will be prosecuted" is meaningless. In the USA things are very different. Not only could you be prosecuted for straying onto private land, but you could be shot, and that is guaranteed to get your attention. I love Britain.

A few other obvious areas of national security where we could be prosecuted for trespass are military bases, chemical and nuclear facilities and the like. And since Michael Fagan managed to get into Buckingham Palace in 1982, and actually have a conversation with Her Majesty while sat on her bed, it is now a criminal offence to trespass in some royal residences.

It's amazing that the only offence Michael Fagan committed at that time was "theft of wine".

Trying for another smile.

There was a young chap who had spent all his life in the Richmond, Chelsea and Camden areas of London. His only experience of the countryside was eating kale and asparagus, and reading stories about animals in his childhood storybooks.

However, he became so impressed with the aerial images of Yorkshire during the Tour de France that he felt compelled to take his life in his hands and see for himself what those people from 'The North' were really like.

He found himself tiptoeing precariously along a country lane near Otley, desperately trying to avoid grass, mud, puddles and unspeakable mounds of things on the lane.

He eventually chanced upon a farmer tending his cow, and he said, "Look here, my good man, why does your cow not have horns?" The farmer doffed his cap politely and said, "Na-then lad, it's like this eer, thasees: sometimes just after t' calf is born we treat thorn root wi chemicals to stop thorn growin'. An sometimes when t' ole milka is gettin a bit cantacrus, we cut thorn off for awer own safety thanose, and sum breeds don't av orns at all, like Angus or Gallaway an tuthers". "But the reason this paticla cow has no orns is cos it's a norse".

Chapter 38: Write it down for future generations, or just for an easy read

Throughout our lives we assume we can continue to ask our parents, guardians and mentors all the questions that come into our heads. Then, before we know it, they are not there to ask.

This was the catalyst to Norky's Ramblings. My dad died in 1990, and since then there has been so many questions I've wanted to ask, not just because I very much enjoyed my time talking to dad about any subject that was fitting to talk about between father and son of our generations, but I could ask more about his war, work, relevant dates, relationships and struggles with bringing up a family.

I wasn't going to make the same mistake with my mum. Therefore, soon after dad died I asked Mum to start writing her memoirs, the following was the result. It is copied direct from Mum's own handwritten words with a few additions by myself in brackets if I thought more explanation was useful.

Mum died in December 1996, she was diagnosed with pancreatic cancer earlier that year, there was nothing more than relief procedures available at that time and she knew that little could be done. Mum was given five months but bravely managed seven. In fact Mum was the bravest person that I have witnessed for myself. She never complained never blamed anybody or anything, always showing her loving and kind nature that was obvious throughout her life.

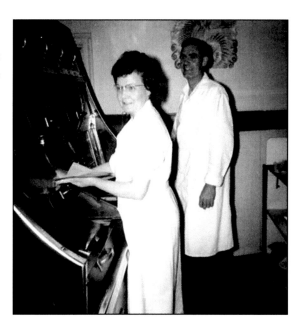

Mum and Dad in their chippy 1966/7,

...and my favourite photo of Mum in her mid seventies.

Chapter 39: Mary Norcliffe. Nee Holdsworth. My Life and Times

I was born Thursday the 13th February 1919, at 135, West Mount, Linthwaite, at 4 o-clock teatime, in the kitchen, in a hurry with mum unattended. I can still remember what our, my elder sister Eva, and my bedroom looked like, also the kitchen and garden, we had a hen hut there, and dad used to tell me about me poking my head into the pop hole and getting stuck. (The pop hole was the opening for the hens to enter and exit). We moved from there when I was two years old, we moved to Handel Street, Golcar where my granddad lived alone.

When my brother Frank was born, dad took Eva and myself to stay with mum's sister Janey. I have just a picture in my mind of a lot of steps leading up to the back door, here is my first memory of music, while walking down a country lane dad broke into singing Lohengrin's "Hail Bright Abode" and "How Sweet are the Breezes".

Music has played an important part in my life. Dad used to help us to sing solos and duets at a very early age, and Saturday nights he played us off to sleep treading the harmoniums and a piano at home, this is real luxury.

I was put into the school choir (Knowl Bank School) when I was eight years old, and stayed there until I left school at 14 years old. I was often given solos to sing when in Sunday school, (Golcar Baptist Chapel) especially at anniversaries. When I was eighteen I asked if I could join the Golcar Baptist choir, the choirmaster was George Stead, In those days we had to sing a test piece to be passed by George, I sang "Arise the Sun" which happens to be a tenor piece, "daft". I stayed in the choir until I married in August 1940, and rejoined when moving back to Golcar in 1983. I was a member of the first U3A choir in Huddersfield, really enjoyable. (U3A - University of the 3rd Age)

I've always loved messing about on the Piano; Dad couldn't afford to pay for lessons until I was 18 years, had six but stopped because I hadn't time to practise and go courting, always regretted this. (Regretted giving up piano lessons, not going courting!)

We lived in Handel Street five years when we moved to 42, Mary Brow in 1924, and lived there for seven years, when we moved into a council house, 18 Ryfields Road, thought we had really gone up in the world.

I got married from there Aug. 3rd. 1940, and gave up a chance of renting a house at Scape (Scapegoat Hill) to go live with Eva, her hubby, Mac, being called up, and my hubby Clifford due to being called up. We thought we would be company for each other, on the whole we were.

By this time there being a great shortage of workforce owing to the conscription of single men and women into the forces, or war work. Part time work was introduced, so war widows, as we called ourselves, could find work to fit in with our times anywhere, whenever we liked, so did quite a few jobs, i.e. cleaning pews down at G.B. Chapel, (Golcar Baptist Chapel) ready for the anniversary, at 2/6 per pew, helping mum's sister, aunty Amy, caretaker at Knowl Bank School, to do holiday cleaning for a lady up Ryefields Road one morning per week.

All these jobs I could take Rhondda who was now a toddler with me.

It all helped to supplement my income of £1/5s (£1.25p) a week forces pay, which was quite a low income, compared to dad's £3 plus he was earning when called up, but he helped by taking every exam he could, which would boost his pay, and then pass on his pay to me.

When Rhondda was eighteen months old, got my first little home at Scapegoat Hill, and moved in August 1944, rent five shilling per month, but income £4/4 shilling per month, not enough to pay for new furniture. Furnished with everything given, bits and pieces, cloth lino on the floor, also utility furniture, thought it was wonderful, felt really proud. Got a job with Eva at Black Rock mill at Linthwaite, taking Rhondda each morning down to my mum's at Golcar, and collected her each evening.

My next move was down to Headwall Green, which contained my first kitchen, but still no bathroom, tin bath in front of the fire Friday nights, starting with youngest of the family and last came dad, muddy by that time. Stayed there about five years, about 1954, got a brand new council house, 76, Longfield Avenue, Golcar, a super home, by that time we could afford all new carpets and downstairs furniture. There I bought my first stairs carpet and Hoover electric washing machine.

I left school Easter 1933, (fourteen years old) I was still recovering from TB and Dr. Hall, our family doctor said mill work wouldn't be suitable, so mum got me a job as a tailoress, but I found it boring, so after a week I went down to Golcar Mill and got a job winding, at a princely sum of five shillings, 25p.

Later that year I moved to John Lockwood's where I earned eleven shillings a week, 55p as a winder, then into the weaving shed as a automatic looms battery filler looking after sixteen looms, the job consisted of keeping all the looms supplied with weft, filling the batteries with bobbins, taking the empty bobbins away, also partly cleaning each loom when empty, and cleaning all sixteen looms on Saturday morning, a filthy job, but had plenty of action, which I liked. That reminds me, a weaving shed is a very noisy place but for some strange reason, I could often hear music and tunes out of the clatter, odd.

Here I learned to weave and after a succession of weaving jobs and at 20 years old I started at B&J Whitwam's, Britannia Road, known locally as Peep. "Peep-o-Day and Edge-o-Dark" half the mill built on one side of the road, day side being in Golcar, and the other side of the road i.e. Linthwaite, known as Edge-o-Dark, because it got little sunshine because it faced north. It was while I worked there the huge main drive wheel on the steam engine broke up, flinging pieces all around the engine room and boiler house, luckily no one was hurt. The owner decided to install electric motors throughout the mill, and I think it would be the first mill down the Colne Valley to be powered by electricity. Left there when I was expecting Rhondda in 1942.

After Rhondda was born I worked at a full time job at B&J Whitwam's, and then Heathhouse, while Rhondda stayed with Aunty Eva during the week, and came home for the weekend, I shared my wage with Eva, who worked at home mending pieces. whilst living with Eva, if Mac came home on leave

I would take Rhondda and myself off to stay with my mum, and Eva and Mac could have the place to themselves, and vice versa when dad was on leave, good old mum, all for no money, just glad to help, Eva doing the same.

Then when Rhondda was three and a half years old, having paid for my furniture and my forces pay now having increased, thanks to Clifford, I decided I could be just about solvent, I could stop working and stay at home with Rhondda. At this point, I must mention my Scape neighbours who were wonderful to me. Aunt Annie, next door, everyone took to us, and we were often invited into neighbours for a meal, and Rhondda would pop in and out of their houses quite often.

(A large section of mum's memoirs dedicated to her time during the war appeared here in her own memoirs, as it featured in my first book 'Norky's Ramblings' it does not need to be repeated again here. However, mum's memoirs go on to included extracts that mum wrote about her three children and our dad)

Rhondda. Not only was it dad's idea to have our first child at that time, but the name, and the spelling was dad's idea entirely, we never did find out why, he took the reason for the name to his grave. Born 8th March 1942, after a 48 hour labour due to her being a big baby (8lbs) and a short cord. In those days the patient's doctor took care during the pregnancy, and then the maternity home, Dr. Hall visited me every day for two weeks, wanted me to stay in hospital more than a week, but no spare beds, Cliff was the first (family member) to see her after myself, having been given sick leave on the Sunday, but could only stay

24 hours, but was home on 7 day leave, just in time to fetch me out of the maternity home. Snow on the ground and bitterly cold day and house when I got home. Rhondda born 5pm Sunday.

Peter. Our first son, and my idea, was born 21st June 1947. He was born at St. Luke's maternity wing in Crosland Moor. A much quicker and easier job. Started labour 2 am on Friday, and was born 5 am the same morning. Some risk of haemorrhage, I didn't know why, but I was ok. None of us could agree on a name, but by some miracle, Cliff and I decided on "Peter" without even discussing it. Rhondda, when hearing she had a baby brother said, "Oh has our Peter come", no one had mentioned the name to her, so it just had to be Peter. Thought of Scott for a second name, wish I had carried it through. A very bonnie baby, after he was born his first cry was accompanied by a pouty lip, which the nurse remarked upon. I never saw the pet lip again. He was a good baby, provided feeds were ready on the dot. He was a very mischievous toddler, wanting to investigate everything, especially the fire. He burnt toys, clothes by throwing them over the fireguard, once that was removed his interest went. Peter had a tonsil op when he was about three. And while waiting in the infirmary outpatients, toddled around and eventually held on to a hot pipe and badly burnt his hand. Wasn't keen on white-coated people for a long time afterwards. He had the usual childish ailments, and recovered quickly from them. Peter had a very strong willpower, and a stubborn streak to go with it, so took quite a bit coping with.

Nicholas was our second son. Born at 76, Longfield Avenue, 10.50 am. 3rd September 1956. A big nine and a half pound lad. There was also a twin that stopped developing at three months.

After which I was terribly uncomfortable. It was quite hard coping with a family, including a new baby whilst Cliff was working night shift.

Nicholas needed Dr. Jameson's help to come into the world. He was a beautiful baby, and very good. Later it was found he had a slight heart murmur, which he had grown out of by the time he was eleven years old. Nicholas had his tonsils removed when he was about five years old.

He spent two or three days in hospital when he was two years old. Any cold etc. sent his temperature up which caused him to have some kind of round (seizure). The check up in hospital proved there was nothing seriously wrong with him. He had the usual childish ailments, measles being the worst, I think he was only about two years old when he had this illness. Nick had a great dislike of injections, and used to go quite faint at the sight of a needle. I'm sure he grew out of this too. His health, after he grew up, seems to have been pretty stable.

Clifford Norcliffe,

I only know when he was young he had a lot of sore throats. He had a tonsil op when he was about 21 years old, that was after I had met him, recovered well. Injured his back during his navy years, and had trouble the rest of his life, he wore a back support corset for many years. He also had a lot of stomach trouble after his navy years, Dr. Hall diagnosed an ulcer, he had one session of three weeks in bed, but after being referred to the infirmary, it was found he had a grumbling appendix, which was removed, afterwards no further stomach trouble. Good health up to July 6th, 1990, when he was admitted into hospital. Then after two thrombosis attacks, a few heart attacks, he passed away six o-clock, July 17th, 1990.

(In mum's memoirs mum wrote here about her holidays, but again they are only interesting to the immediate family. However there is one section below that I thought may be of interest).

July 5th 1993, I saw a six-day-old baby girl this morning, brought out by her mother, the baby was wearing a dress, long cardigan, socks and a knitted beret. When I compare it to the baby clothes we wore, there is such a difference. During the day baby would wear something called a barras, a long winceyette under gown with a vest like top and a long skirt, under that would be a vest, and over would be a long cotton nightdress with embroidery and something lace, over this would be worn a matinee jacket, the cotton nightdress would be replaced by a flannelette one for night wear. All this would be worn for a year, (washed regularly of course) when the baby was put into shorts clothes for the first time. This was known as shortening, and was done with great fuss and family ceremony.

One aspect of Mum's life I thought I would expand upon a little. As mentioned previously mum was born in the kitchen of 135 West Mount, Linthwaite at 4 o'clock in the afternoon. Her mum Maggie was unattended at the time. Luckily my mum was Maggie's third child, so the procedure probably wasn't completely unfamiliar, but I'm sure it wasn't an ideal situation. Maggie just kept herself and the newborn baby Mary warm and comfortable until help arrived. Apart from Granddad Edward's tea not being on the table when he got home from work, all was well. It wasn't unusual at that time and certainly previous generations for that 'help' to be a neighbour or family member, childbirth was so familiar and almost an everyday occurrence that there was usually a local lady who could be called upon to act as midwife.

Several people wrote about poverty and the lives of the poor. Some notables being Charles James Booth 1840–1916, John Ernest Steinbeck 1902–1968 and Charles John Huffam Dickens 1812–1870. However, in my humble opinion, the most notable writer of social interaction was Eric Arthur Blair 1903–1950, better known as George Orwell.

All of these writers wrote about the lives of the common people, but few, if any, actually experienced real poverty and a lifetime of starvation. And of course, all could write. Nothing was written by the people actually experiencing these conditions. If they were lucky enough to have a reasonable basic education that enabled them to read and write, they would have little opportunity to do so in later life.

Much of the social support, solace and comfort for the poor came from religion and music. And much of the music was religious performed in churches and chapels throughout the country, where the congregation could also mix with likeminded people from an equally poor background where they could be comforted by sermons and stories about people similar to themselves.

My mum, Mary Norcliffe née Holdsworth, gained much comfort from both religion and music. She was a lifelong Golcar Baptist Church supporter and sang in several choirs. Her father Edward

Holdsworth (Ned 'o' Jims) was an organist and choirmaster and passed on his musical enthusiasm to his children and many of his grandchildren

Norky's Ramblings are meant as an expanded version of what mum wrote above. I would highly recommend that we ask all our older generations to write their own memoirs. Like my own Norky's Ramblings they may be insignificant and mean nothing in the larger scheme of things. However, at some time they may become interesting to somebody. In my case they are a reflection of a humble working family, just trying to get by.

Chapter 40: Local sites and regular visitors to Golcar and Bolster Moor

Bolster Moor taken from Scapegoat Hill, Photograph by Graham Butler.

The Golcar Lily restaurant is in the foreground. Just a few yards further along Slades Road is a small commission weaving and mending company, now demolished to make way for housing. Further along again is Sunny Bank Chapel, and at the top of the road nestling in the trees is Headwall Green where my early memories were formed. Across from the Golcar Lily is the posh stone and tiled roof bus shelter where I used to pick Moi up on the bike, if I hadn't fallen off or been stopped by the police.

During my early childhood soon after WW2, life in the villages of Bolster Moor and Golcar was very quiet, predictable and on the whole peaceful. Rationing was still very much dictating our everyday lives, although, as a child, I wasn't aware of the difficulties involved. I was just happy to be fed.

Some basic things like meat were still rationed right up to 1954. One thing that we all regard now as a staple is bread, and although this was never rationed during the war, it was for a short time in 1946. Fruit and vegetables were never rationed during the war either, but were often in short supply. Because of this, and to eliminate some of the need to import these items, the government encouraged a 'grow your own' attitude. Many back gardens were turned over (literally) to growing spuds, onions, sprouts, green beans, turnips, rhubarb, celery and of course cabbages. Allotments sprang up everywhere, and many municipal parks were utilised for the same need.

Even though there were difficulties, life was simple and, in many ways, predictable. During the previous wartime years, parents had become accustomed to hardships, and had developed a 'make do and mend' way of life, but at least in the late forties and fifties, we were not at war.

The sights, sounds and people we saw around the village were also very predictable. Wagons, busses, tractors and horses were common but there were very few cars. The local family doctor would be one of the very few people around the village who had one. Doctors were also the only people with a telephone. However, there were public telephone boxes dotted around in every village.

This was the Bolster Moor phone box only a few years ago.
Alas now gone along with most of the others.

We have a bench, waste bin and bus shelter now, so all is not lost.

Other predictable characters around the villages included our milkman, who delivered milk using a pony and trap, pulled by a black and white horse. He would ladle milk from a large milk churn into a jug that mum put on the doorstep. No more than a pint at a time as there was no way of keeping it for more than a day, and often not even that long.

We would also see the same predictable postman every day on his rounds. Children very rarely spoke to adults in the street, both parties knowing that children had nothing to contribute. However, when I was reaching an age of self-consciousness – I would be about ten years old – probably following the visit by Christa from Germany, described in a previous 'Puberty' ramble, I had a memorable encounter with our regular postman.

He approached me in the street and, as I saw him advance towards me, I thought he was going to ask me something so important that my answer would surely improve his day immensely. What he said was, "Your fly's open", and then he walked on. I was speechless with embarrassment, so much so that I remember it vividly to this day. I have no idea why, as he didn't say it in a creepy or mocking way. I blame Christa. Puberty was a very strange time for me, and I suspect for many others. I'm sure I must be nearly through it now.

Other regulars were the council rent man each week, and the Prudential insurance collector, probably once a month. Another regular was the rag and bone man, on yet another horse and cart. Think of Steptoe and Son, and you won't be far off. He would shout "Ahhn o ahhhs". I assume it was "Any old rags" but it was never closer than "Ahhn o ahhhs". The rags were proper rags, nothing fit to wear or pass down of course, all destined for the rag pulling mills.

If he was impressed with our modest offering, he would give us a goldfish in a plastic bag. Unfortunately, the rag and bone men gave away goldfish with a "best before date" of the day before.

Other characters around the village, particularly on the Sycamore Avenue estate were the police, usually walking – yes, walking – in pairs. Each parish had its own police station serving the local public. There were also many of those little blue police boxes dotted around somewhere on their beat, a very rare sight now. One such box was made famous as the Tardis in the BBC's series *Doctor Who*.

Of course, we exaggerated the flaysome (frightening) reputation of our local rozzers (police). We convinced ourselves that they would give us a whack with their capes without provocation, even suggesting to ourselves that they sewed little lead weights into the hem of the cape for added probability of unconsciousness for anybody who dared to stand close enough. They always wore their tall hats of course and often sported a large military moustache. Along with the dark navy uniform, and that cape, the overall impression was of "Don't mess with us, matey".

Sergeant Snell was our local bobby, and he seemed quite pleasant when we saw him in his garden proudly pruning his roses. But put him in his uniform and there was definitely no messing with him.

Our parents, and particularly the police themselves, encouraged and probably enjoyed this reputation. If we psychologically convince ourselves that if we messed with a particular individual or group, we will come off second best, then we will inevitably come off second best. Moreover, if we were stupid enough to be noticed by the police, we would run the risk of being frog-marched back home for another dressing down from our parents, who would never contemplate questioning the officer who had us by the scruff of the neck. As the officer lived among and knew most of the people in the village it was likely that they knew where the little scruff lived.

I remain unconvinced that what we have now is better. Our disciplined, 'make do and mend' and 'life can be a right bugger' attitude following WW2 has eroded, now, we question too much and we are never to blame.

I think there is still a place for two burly, moustachioed, tall hatted, honest, pillar of the community police officers who are allowed to use common sense and initiative, and who last long enough in the job to become experienced, unlike the spotty faced university graduates who last just long enough to make a mark on their CV.

Bring back the coppers with lead weights in their capes patrolling our streets. Who but the ne'er-do-well would not sleep better at night?

Chapter 41: Time to talk about prostates

When a man, that is a person with a prostate, ...I know that others have a slightly different opinion whether a prostate is exclusively found within the male human, but in my humble opinion that is where it resides and anybody who thinks differently is delusional at best or just a daft apeth. (half penny)

Anyway, when this man reaches the age of about 50 to 60, nature and in particular your family doctor becomes less interested in your genitalia and develops an unhealthy interest in our anus and rectum. I'm sure there is a female equivalent, but I can only speak from my own experience.

There was an incident when I was 64 years old that prompted me to ask my doctor about my blood sugars. He duly took a blood sample, and a few days later informed me that my sugars were fine but my cholesterol and PSA (prostate specific antigens) were high. I made an appointment to ascertain how he knew, knowing that I didn't like the screening systems and had refused all previous screening options.

As I was most dissatisfied with the answer (standard procedure) I duly blamed the messenger for my slightly high good cholesterol and a PSA figure of 46. The acceptable figure at that time for someone of my age was 5. The acceptable figure now is even less. I then shot the messenger and was transferred to my mate's surgery, the Major of the W.A.R.T.S. walking group, who in turn gave me a right bollocking for blaming someone who had probably saved my life, and he has never allowed me to forget it ever since. On and on and on he goes.

Up to that point in my life, I had not developed a need for my anus to be used for anything but an outlet pipe. I believe there are other views available, but not in my case. However, for a few months after this diagnosis the medical profession were queuing up to examine my poor old prostate, which meant going up the exit pipe. The biopsy samples and then the following treatment were all carried out from the same area. The biopsy included a local anaesthetic which was relatively straight forward, all be it with bleeding for a few days.

The oncologist (cancer specialist) advised "brachytherapy" which is a type of radiotherapy whereby a radiation pellet is placed in or near the cancer site. This included a five-hour full anaesthetic, and at least three specialists, I say three based on the number of people that came to see me just before the procedure. Each one came in individually and each one asking for my identity, date of birth and so on. I was beginning to ask myself, "surely no-one else would want to go through this?"

Luckily, I had, or have had no idea what they got up to back there, but apparently part of the procedure included a camera, a computer controlled aiming system and several guided missiles, all probably adding up to the size of a table leg. I don't think my poor little bum has ever been the same since. I'm glad to say that after those first few months all interest by the medical profession in my bum ceased, and I can't say I'm surprised. It must have been in a right state by then.

However, the treatment continued with hormone therapy for a further three years. Apparently prostate cancer thrives on testosterone. I'm sure many ladies will say the testosterone is responsible for many detrimental issues within the male body, prostate cancer is just another one.

After the first three months on hormone treatment I began to notice changes in my body. My head hair grew thicker and more lush, my body hair almost disappeared and my breasts grew, not to magnificent proportions whereby I could earn a living as a fairground attraction or in the film industry, but they certainly grew bigger than before. I also developed a liking for Rosé Wine, I had totally forgotten the off-side rule in kickerball and couldn't for the life in me, park the car.

Six months after finishing my three-year hormone treatment I reverted back to some sort of normality, for right or wrong. The jury's still out.

All this sounds horrendous, and I'm sure many ladies who have experienced pregnancy, childbirth, and many other procedures and screening, may say, "Think yourself lucky matey". But even for me, the experience wasn't as bad as my imagination beforehand led me to believe. Unfortunately or fortunately, depending how we see it, I didn't have any symptoms, it was found in a routine screening that I was stupidly offended by at the time.

In my humble opinion, when us chaps get to a certain age, or if there are other chaps in the family with prostate problems, we should discuss it with our doctors, or each other. We just have to grit our teeth for a while and bite the bullet, and any other cliché that may help, and get on with it. At least we have a very good chance of a healthy long life, and our doctor will take less interest in our genitalia.

Luckily there is no image available for this particular ramble.

I plan to live forever, and as of writing this in 2022, so far so good. The last chapter may indicate my most recent attempts to hide from The Grim  .